Nostalgic
Barnsley

The publishers would like to thank the following companies for their support in the production of this book

Main sponsor
Premier Foods PLC

Barnsley College

Barnsley Lock & Safe Co. Ltd

Barnsley MBC Town Centre & Market Services

Brian Totty Signs & Design Ltd

C. Soar & Sons

Dimensions - The Barnsley Hairdressing Company

Jakto Transport Ltd

Koyo Bearings (Europe) Ltd

The Rack Group Ltd

Ron Daley (Motorcycles) Ltd

Naylor Industries

First published in Great Britain by True North Books Limited
England HX3 6SN
01422 244555

ISBN 978 - 1906649296

Text, design and origination by True North Books
Printed and bound by The Amadeus Press

Nostalgic *Barnsley*

CONTENTS

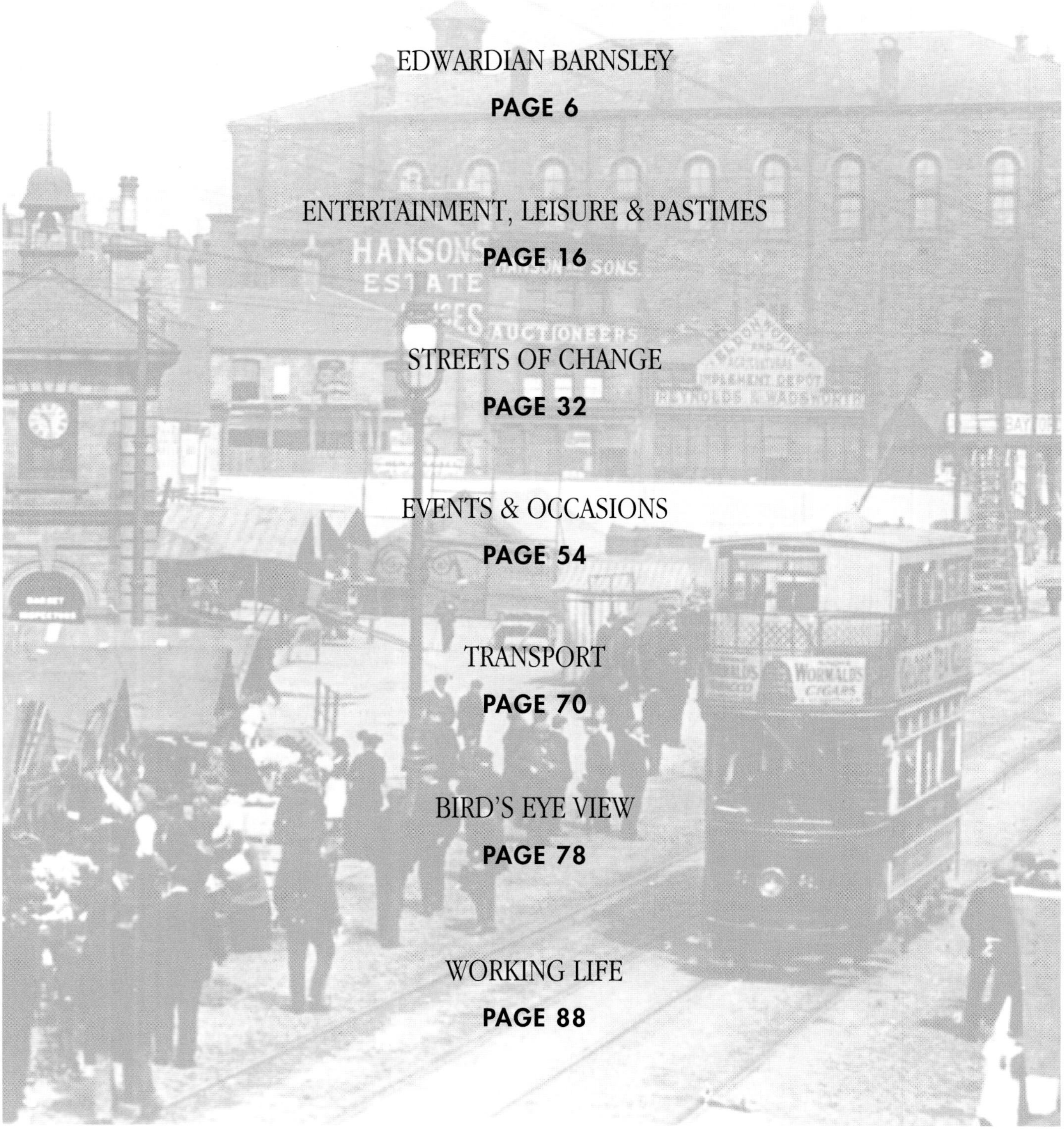

EDWARDIAN BARNSLEY

PAGE 6

ENTERTAINMENT, LEISURE & PASTIMES

PAGE 16

STREETS OF CHANGE

PAGE 32

EVENTS & OCCASIONS

PAGE 54

TRANSPORT

PAGE 70

BIRD'S EYE VIEW

PAGE 78

WORKING LIFE

PAGE 88

INTRODUCTION

There are a number of English towns that have their own particular sense of identity. Barnsley is one such place. At first glance, it would appear to be just another north country spot that once relied upon mining for its economy and has now slipped back even further into mediocrity. But, that would be far from the truth. Its glassmaking enterprises still flourish and the town centre boasts a number of impressive projects that include the new Interchange, the digital media centre, Gateway Plaza, the Markets Complex and Experience Barnsley, the museum and archive centre. The town is also celebrated for its impressive Town Hall and influential College, one of the largest educational establishments in Europe. Recreation and culture feature strongly in the locality, with sport represented by such stars as Test cricketer Darren Gough and umpire Harold 'Dickie' Bird, soccer's Mick McCarthy, the Greenhoff brothers, David Hirst and the late Mark Jones and Tommy Taylor, two of the original Busby Babes. We can also rejoice in the achievements of Olympic sprinter Dorothy Hyman. Barnsley supports a variety of music, from its prestigious brass bands to the folk songs of Kate Rusby and the heavy metal of Saxon. Trade union leader Arthur Scargill and the writer/broadcaster Michael Parkinson hail from the town that was mentioned over 900 years ago in the Domesday Book as 'Berneslai', a word said by many to mean a field barn.

'Nostalgic Barnsley' is a book that traces the development of the borough through the last century by bringing to the reader a collection of glorious photographs, accompanied by text intended to stimulate thoughts and comments about times gone by. They are the decades through which some of us have lived or that we have heard about from our parents and grandparents. Within these pages are moments when young men walked on the outside of their girlfriends as they went along the street. They lifted their hats when greeting a lady and offered their seats on a bus as it was bad form to let one of the fairer sex stand when she could sit. We make no excuses for being nostalgic about these days of yesteryear.

As the reader goes from page to page, he will be reminded of the day when he spent his money in bobs, tanners and half crowns. Fruit and vegetables were bought by the ounce and pound and footballers were centre forwards and not strikers. We drove black Morris Cowleys and Austin Sevens rather than midnight pink, or whatever, Japanese, German or Korean cars. The seaside was 75 miles away, not 120 kilometres. We should cherish our heritage more than ever, and, remember what we had on our own doorstep as it helped mould the society in which we find ourselves today. Inside this book are memories of May Day Green when Paige's fashions were all the rage or you could check what was on offer at Hunter's Tea Store. We can think back to walking down Regent Street when Needs and Company offered accountancy advice or WH Gelder ran a plumbing and electrical business. Transistor radios played 'I Like it' by Gerry and the Pacemakers and the crowds at Oakwell wept as our lads tasted Division Four for the first time.

Not everything about the past can be viewed as being rosy. There were many instances of hardship and poverty to be found in Barnsley. Yet, with true Yorkshire grit, we survived and flourished. Looking through 'Nostalgic Barnsley' we see many smiling faces and children of the time playing safely on Barnsley streets. The companies and organisations which have developed and thrived in the city over the recent decades are many. We take pleasure in including in this book histories of an outstanding selection of different companies whose contribution to the development and sustainability of the town's economic prosperity is a matter of record. With their co-operation and access to their respective photographic archives, we have been able to tell their stories and hopefully trigger the memories of local people who have worked for them or been touched by their part in community life. So, sit down and relax with a glass of Clarkson's best ale and listen out for the call of the rag and bone man. It is time for a few, fond memories.

TEXT	ANDREW MITCHELL
PHOTOGRAPH COMPILATION	TONY LAX
DESIGNER	SEAMUS MOLLOY
BUSINESS DEVELOPMENT EDITOR	PETER PREST

EDWARDIAN BARNSLEY

A much changed view looking up Market Hill not many years before the outbreak of World War I, just a single isolated van can be spotted alongside the stall on the left. The horse and cart bowling over the cobbled setts was still as familiar a sight as any motorised transport. Of course, that was to change rapidly over the next few years as four legs gave way to four wheels. Smart men in their boaters and working men under their flat caps went about their business under the watchful gaze of a couple of custodians of the law. The bobby in the centre foreground was there to help keep moving what traffic there was, but also to help keep the peace. On market day, it had been known for disputes to break out around the pitches if accusations of short changing or inaccurate weighing were bandied about. It was also a good place for pickpockets to practise their so called art. The man in uniform outside the Yorkshire Penny Bank may have been stationed there on a specific duty in case a cash delivery was due. Stories of bank robberies in America were well chronicled and we did not want any of that wild west nonsense in Yorkshire, thank you very much. We liked our villains to stick to fiddles rather than machine guns in violin cases, as would become the scene across the Atlantic in the next couple of decades.

Above: A group of children dressed up for 'ale and cake day' on Maundy Thursday in Penistone around 1900. The word "maundy" may have come from the maund (or mand) basket used by the fishermen in the English counties of Norfolk and Suffolk. Centuries ago, there was a fair held on this day in Norwich, at which vendors sold horses, cattle and general merchandise. Some of the fisher-folk brought their maund baskets filled with items to sell, including fish. Clothing and hats were sold, as it was customary to buy a new item of clothing for Easter Sunday. This may well have been the origin of the Easter bonnet and the notion of wearing new spring attire for Easter. Maundy Thursday may also have come from the Latin word "mandatum," meaning "commandment," as in the Biblical words of Jesus. Although many Easter customs continue to this day, this particular one was discontinued in 1905.

Right: You could not call out 'Get your skates on' to hurry these children along, seen here posing for a photograph outside the Olympia Skating Rink. A different type of footwear was needed and yelling, 'Get your rollers on' did not have the same meaning. Roller skates were first seen in the 18th century, but the first patented design was not registered until 1819. The earliest models lacked manoeuvrability and directional changes could only be made by using wide, sweeping turns. The four-wheeled turning skate was invented in New York in 1863 and developed in Britain in the 1870s with the inclusion of ball bearing races that gave the skates even greater mobility. Daring young things loved showing off their prowess and dedicated centres opened in growing numbers at the turn of the century. The Olympia rink began business in 1909, but the wave of interest in silent movies, with such headliners as Rudolph Valentino, Douglas Fairbanks, Mary Pickford and Lilian Gish, meant that its success was shortlived. Audiences wanted to be entertained, rather than provide for themselves an escape from the boredom of mundane life. The film industry grew massively as techniques improved and people could not wait to get their next taste of action, accompanied by the twinkling fingers of a pianist who provided mood music to accompany the action on the silver screen. The Olympia was kitted out with the best seats and the finest décor and renamed the Pavilion Cinema in 1920. It was gutted by fire 30 years later.

Above: Dating from a century ago, the picture of Penistone livestock market is a vivid reminder of how different day to day life was for our grandparents and great grandparents. The rapid technological strides made over the last 100 years have brought us aeroplanes, motorcars, radio, television, computers and countless other aids to daily life. But the camera shows us that, in comparatively recent times, we still relied heavily on the land and traditional farming and rural activities to run our daily lives. There were sheep pens in front of the Spread Eagle pub. The market was also the place for the local 'hirings' of young men and women to work on local farms and in farmhouses. Although declining in importance as the years went by, livestock sales continued until quite late in the 20th century. Trading in open markets such as this one had been a commonplace feature of all towns and villages for a millennium. In a way, there is still a link now with these old days as a general auction is often held at this very place and a farmers' market is a regular feature in the nearby retail market area.

Top right: Hemsworth relied heavily on coal for its prosperity, though that is far from obvious in this scene from over a century ago when Limbert's mobile fruit and vegetable business stopped to sell produce on Market Street. St Helen's Parish Church, in the background, had a Norman nave until Victorian times when reconstruction work was undertaken by John L Pearson. He was an architect who was also involved with developments on the cathedrals in Lincoln and Truro. The old yew tree in the churchyard has, at its base, an inscribed tablet mentioning that it lost some of its branches in a gale in 1884. St Helen was the mother of Constantine the Great. She is generally credited with finding relics of the true Cross of Christ.

Right: William Ayrton brewed his own ales for the Flying Dutchman, on Cemetery Road. Many pubs relied on their own individual brews or bought in beers from small, local

concerns. The mighty behemoths of the industry were yet a long way off, thank goodness. This carefully posed snapshot of life over a century ago suggests not just a different era, but one of which we have little comprehension. What would it have been like when the horse was dominant? How did families manage to exist on just a few shillings a week and how did they get along in homes that lacked electricity and hot water? We can only guess.

Right: Dating from the early years of the last century, this charming picture shows a group of infants happily playing on Sheffield Road. They have been completely ignored by the man in the three piece suit and his pipe smoking companion. Although there was a slight risk that a horse and cart might come bowling along the cobblestones, youngsters did not have to worry about motorcars in those days. Scuffed knees would appear to be the only calamity to befall them.

Below: The car belonging to the Barnsley Electric Tram Company made its way from Kendray Street via Eldon Street on a market day in 1911. The service first ran in 1902 with a fleet of just 10 vehicles. The fares charged were equivalent to about a penny per mile and were good value. They revolutionised the way the general public thought of going into town. In earlier times, it was

almost something of a pilgrimage for those living on the outskirts. For others it was a route march, but the wonder of electricity brought the centre of Barnsley so much nearer in terms of time. You could get there and back, having completed your shopping on the Market, in a matter of a few, short hours. Beforehand, it was a full day of a job. Within a few years of opening for business, the electric tramway was carrying 2 million passengers per year. It carried on serving the public along this route until the summer of 1930, when motorbuses took over. This part of town was completely remodelled in the 1970s and Kendray Street became May Day Green. Hanson's Auctioneers, the Eldon Works and the Cross Keys Hotel were consigned to the memory banks. Some of the so called improvements included the dreaded concrete blocks that only the planners of that period found attractive. To the rest of us, they are significant blots on what was once a pleasant landscape. The new Kendray Street was built as an approach to the railway crossing.

Above: The austerely dressed women in the left foreground contrasted greatly with the attire and demeanour of those on the other side of Kendray Street, outside the Wellington Hotel close to May Day Green. The more brightly dressed ladies with the toddler appeared much more modern in their choice of dresses, though the skirt lengths that brushed the ground still conformed to the strictures of polite society in late Victorian times. Those dressed in black may well have been widows as it was commonplace for such bereaved ladies to continue to advertise their loss for the rest of their lives, copying the example of the Queen who mourned her beloved Albert for 40 years. Even so, it is strange that such fashions should have been clung to on streets that were far from the cleanest that one would like to encounter. The open market stalls seemed to be doing good business and traders were continuing a practice that had been carried out since the 13th century when monks from Pontefract began selling their wares in the town. The market grew until it was the largest open air one in the north of England.

Right: Horse manure rather than diesel spillage was the problem on our roads in the early 1900s. Only the occasional motorcar chugged by and such a grand tourer as this one in the centre of the frame was a real head turner and talking point. Something of a small charabanc rather than just a motor car, the model we see here in Peel Street around 1912, had room for about 10 passengers. It was a bit cramped and rather draughty, but they were cheap prices to pay for the pleasure of being the centre of attention, the object of everyone's envy and having fun in the open air. With its vehicle registration plate of DB 59, we know that it came originally from Manchester. Having such identification of a vehicle lodged and displayed became mandatory at the start of 1904. Using just two initial letters was sufficient until 1932 when the stock of available permutations was becoming exhausted. A third letter was introduced and this solved problems, along with a reversal of letters and numbers in some areas, until 1963 when a suffix letter had to be deployed.

Below: Proctor's Pavilion Picture Variety Palace was something of a mouthful for most Wombwell folk to get their teeth around. Consequently, most just referred to it as the Pavilion. Situated on Marsh Street, the site has been put to several uses over the years. Having been a successful picture house and cinema, it went the way of most of its type in the second half of the last century when it was turned into a bingo hall. In more recent times it has seen something of a reincarnation as Wombwell Snooker and Social Club.

Below: The smoking chimneys, belching out their noxious fumes, were not much of a backdrop to the 1912 Penistone Show. This was a normal sight of the times and never going to put locals off enjoying the fun of the fair, with its sideshows, stalls, roundabouts and speciality tents. Novelty acts, such as the bearded lady and the wild man from Borneo, made punters' eyes pop out of their heads. Little did they know that the whiskers were held in place by fish glue and that the untamed savage was also known as Harold to his missus in Castleford. Still, even if they did, it was all good fun. There was a boxing booth where young swains could try to impress the ladies with their prowess in the ring. More often than not they were unceremoniously dumped on the seat of their pants by a hard bitten pro whose broken nose and cauliflower ears reflected a tough way of earning a living. The first Penistone Show was held in mid Victorian times and still thrives today as one of South Yorkshire's premier annual agricultural shows.

ENTERTAINMENT, LEISURE & PASTIMES

Modern day children have just about everything they need lavished upon them and lead very high-tech and designer labelled lives. They would probably think that the boys and girls in these photographs were from another planet, as their lives were so different. Yet, they are only a few generations away. We can go back to those times if we really use our imaginations and personal memory banks. Thankfully, there are old photographs like this one from Silkstone, grainy film, written records and objects from those days to which we can refer. Living museums at Elsecar, Beamish and other centres help us recapture a bit of what it was like to grow up at the end of Victoria's reign or during Edwardian times.

In the early 1900s, times were a-changing, as Bob Dylan would put it in the 1960s. Better conditions were on the horizon, with new sewage systems and electricity being installed in towns and villages. Medical care improved and there was schooling for everyone to help even the poorest get an education of sorts. Many children in early Victorian England never went to school at all and more than half of them grew up unable even to read or write. But, after the Education Act of 1870, all children from five to thirteen had to attend school by law. Lessons concentrated on the 'three Rs', with writing being carried out on slates that were wiped clean and used over and over again. Small misdemeanours were punished by a caning from the teacher. However, the lessons gave children the tools with which they could compete with the more privileged in a small way in later life.

Playtime was great. This was when there was a break from learning and shrieking children could let off steam in a small yard next to the schoolroom. As well as chasing and catching games, they played blind mans' buff, snakes and ladders, cowboys and Indians, hide and seek, hopscotch and skipping. Some boys would beg a pig's bladder from the butcher, which they would blow up to use as a football. Others drilled hob nails through cotton reels to make spinning tops. When they got back home, children played happily in the street and ginnels at the back of their houses. There were no motorcars roaring down the road for them to worry about. All they had to do was make sure that they did not kick a ball against Mrs Shacklady's front door as she had a short fuse and was not averse to giving them a clip round the ear. Of course it was no good complaining to your dad about being assaulted by a neighbour as he would tell you that you deserved it and wallop you himself for good measure.

scratched in the earth, wally, when a glass 'alley' was bounced off a backdrop, and many others. In this last one, the two dips in a manhole cover were used as targets. In the late autumn, it was time for conkers. There were certain rules to be observed in connection with soaking in vinegar or baking in an oven. Cries of, 'I've got a forty five-er' were nothing to do with guns, but the conker success rate. Throughout the year, hoops were bowled along with sticks. Hopscotch squares were chalked on the ground, brightly coloured tops were whipped and backs arched in games of leapfrog. The street lamppost was used as the wicket in a game of cricket and a couple of dustbins or piles of coats sufficed as goalposts for football. Girls played two ball and chanted rhymes about salt, vinegar, mustard and pepper as they threw. They played 'knock down ginger', much to the annoyance of those in a nearby street on whose door they

The street games that youngsters played showed a mix of imagination and ingenuity. They were expected to entertain themselves. There was no money for expensive toys and the adults were too busy to set anything up for them. Some of the pastimes were seasonal. There seemed to be a special time when marbles were all the rage. You could play various types of marble game. There was ring-o, where a circle was

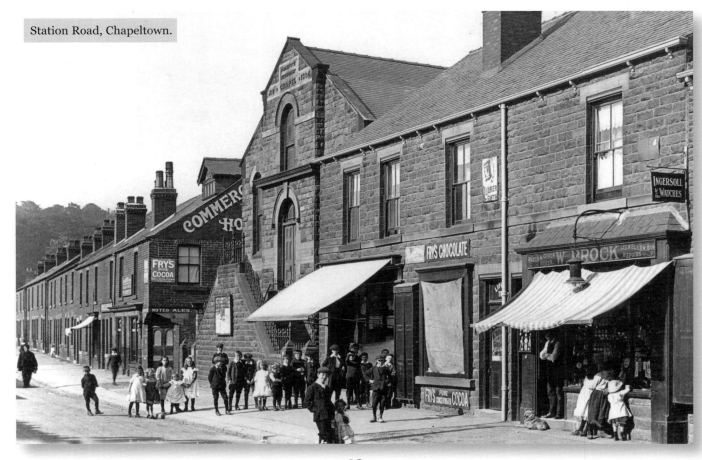

Station Road, Chapeltown.

grandpa's loft and see if you can find a pack of playing cards that has the title 'Happy Families' or 'Old Maid' on the cover. Look through grandma's trunk and find her old miniature tea service. Sit teddy, golly and the other dollies down and serve them with an imaginary cuppa. Nothing to do? Don't be silly. Just pretend that you were born in 1900 and there is tons of entertainment out there, but you must help make most of it yourself. The congregation of children with dirty knees in the top photograph are from Newstead Avenue, Fitzwilliam, and the kiddies below belong to the baby boomer generation that dates from just after the last war. Pictured in a backyard in Railway View, Goldthorpe, in 1953.

banged before running off. They dare not do it on their own patch where they were known or justice would have been instant and painful. 'What's the time Mr Wolf?' or 'What's my trade?' were just a couple of other larger group games that were played.

So, 21st century young 'un, nothing to do? Pack up your battery powered, remote controlled Batmobile. Instead, root in

Above: Pictured around c1930, this joint outing by churchgoers from Mapplewell and Staincross had brought them to the seaside for a day out. Such trips were special occasions and the journey from home to the sea front was undertaken by coach or train. Few members of the working classes had the wherewithal to afford a private motorcar. Such extravagance was for the middle classes. So, they came in their droves with the avowed intention of making the most of the day before they had to return to the coal face or factory floor once again. They dressed up for the occasion and the best suits, hats, frocks and coats came out of the wardrobes. Down on the sand, they made a bee-line for the deckchairs. Hang the expense. It was well worth a couple of pence to be able to sit on that piece of canvas for the next six hours. Just pass the sandwiches, mother, and we will enjoy our time watching the waves lap on the shore as the seagulls whirl overhead. Never mind if we suffer from cramp or the wind blows as keenly as ever onshore from the east. The trippers had their little bit of escapism from the daily grind. Some of the more intrepid souls chanced using a bucket and spade or went for a walk along the prom. Most, though, sat there stoically and steadfastly, defying the elements to spoil their fun.

Below: Once you had claimed your square yard of sand, that was it for the day, come hell, high water or the occasional rainstorm. Deckchairs were erected, albeit with some difficulty as the contraptions always seemed to have a knack of taking a chunk out of your fingers. The kids scrabbled around in the sand

with their buckets and spades and mum smiled benignly and offered little bits of advice or warnings about making sure they knew where the family was if they wandered off. The menfolk gazed out to sea passively, just happy that they had a week away from the shop floor. If the sun shone, those with flat caps were fine. They pulled them out of their pockets and plonked them squarely on their heads. It was the hatless ones who provided their own peculiar fashion statements. Whatever the temperature, the jacket stayed firmly in place, but the head was protected in a variety of ways. Some opted for the hankie, with a knot tied at each corner. Then there was the tea towel. Quite how this managed to get itself packed is a mystery, but it found its way onto the beach year after year. The newspaper made a good titfer. Either opened at the middle page and placed aloft or carefully crafted into a Robin Hood style by the use of South Yorkshire origami, it did its job.

Above: Does my bum look big in this? This lass has all the potential for giving lads a tough time. Not only is she very pretty, but she also knows it. Look out, boys. She was obviously well aware of modern fashion. Her modern, knitted two piece was designed more to catch the eye than for practical purposes. The fabric would have got rather heavy and sag somewhat when immersed in the sea. Anyway, she was more interested in making waves among the males on the sands. The first modern two piece was created by Louis Réard in 1946, naming it the bikini after the atoll where atomic bomb tests were carried out. Réard reasoned that the costume's effects would be akin to that of a nuclear reaction and he was not far wrong. It blew some men's brains apart. However, more modest two piece costumes, like the one seen here, had been modelled in the early 1940s by such movie stars as Ava Gardner, Lana Turner and Rita Hayworth. This lovely on the golden sands could dream that she was in the same league as those doyennes of the silver screen.

Rising in Yorkshire, in the midst of the beautiful Peak District National Park, the River Don flows for 70 miles through Sheffield and the Pennines until it meets the River Ouse at Goole. The surrounding countryside is, at times, simply breathtaking. This part of Yorkshire is known for its steep hills, which means that energetic visitors can enjoy panoramic views of the Don valley from several high vantage points. Penistone and Thurgoland boast particularly pleasing rural settings. In urban centres such as Rotherham and Doncaster, the Don valley still bears traces of industry. But the Don of today is a clean and healthy river, which salmon, trout and grayling are happy to call home. This idyllic snow scene of the River Don was taken near Thurgoland. The picture is not dated but until recently, one of the worst snowfalls on record in South Yorkshire was in 1940, when 120 centimetres of snow fell in two days, at the end of January.

Left: An inscription on this 1938 photograph states that the ceremony for the official opening of the Recreation Ground at Millhouse Green was conducted by 'Mr Anson, an old master'. Presumably this meant that the gentleman in question was a former teacher rather than a distinguished oil painting. The play area belongs to the village that is on the A628, just west of Penistone. Let us hope that the children made full use of the roundabout and swings as there would not be much in the way of fun and games for them beyond these railings in the coming years. By the time that Mr Anson cut the ceremonial tape, Hitler's forces had already annexed Austria and threats about the future of Czechoslovakia had been made. The storm clouds of war that everyone talked about began to gather. The children in the village would, though, be among the luckier ones. Their rural setting would protect them from the carnage wreaked upon the major towns and cities in the early 1940s when Goering's Luftwaffe flew overhead.

Below: The Yorkshire Naturalists' Union is a registered charity and umbrella organisation for smaller groups with similar interest and ideals. The Union shows particular interest in the study and welfare of birds, herpetiles, insects, mammals, molluscs, fungi, mosses and plants. In other words, it is concerned with anything living in natural surroundings in the wild. Barnsley has its own Naturalist and Scientific Society that was founded in 1867. It meets fortnightly in the town library and organises regular weekend field trips. Many of the events organised by the Yorkshire Union are also extremely well patronised. The visit to Worsbrough Reservoir and Rockley Woods on 21 May, 1949, attracted a large number of participants, as do similar ventures today. The reservoir was built as one of the feeders to the Dearne and Dove Canal that opened to traffic in 1799. There is very little left of the waterway which closed over a century ago, but the lake area and surrounding parkland are popular with visitors and anglers. The wetland at the western end is well used by birdwatchers, while children can enjoy tossing crusts to the ducks and geese. Rockley Woods, parts of which are now known as Bell Bank Wood, Birdwell Wood and Old Park Wood, belonged to an ancient forest that once covered most of Rockley Valley. Deer were hunted there in Norman times.

Above and below: On high days and holidays we put on our best frocks and smartest suits and made sure that the girls had ribbons in their hair and the boys' knees were well scrubbed. It was the period in our social history when the 'charrer' was the magic carpet that would carry us off to distant shores. These tended to be Blackpool or Bridlington rather than the more exotic Black Sea but, compared with our back streets, they were paradise. Usually, the coaches were filled with people who knew one another.

They would be from the same church group or neighbourhood. Sometimes, a pub would organise an outing for its regulars or a works would sponsor a seaside run as a reward for its workforce. Few people could afford motorcars, so this was the way whole families went off for the day. The journeys were not always to a coastal resort, as there were mystery tours of the countryside that might involve a stop at a country

house or an attraction such as Trentham Gardens that became very popular either side of the last war. However, the kiddies often felt cheated if they had to endure a 'posh house' or 'boring flower beds'. So, it tended to be a case of pointing the nose of the charabanc towards the sea and off we go. The starting handle on the Dennis coach is a real throwback to yesteryear. Some of us can still recall dad swinging on that piece of equipment while mum pumped the accelerator in an effort to get the engine to turn over. We can also remember the cry of, 'Don't flood it, woman!' followed by some icy retort from our normally long-suffering mother.

Below: In 1950, before the 'telly' dominated our living rooms, people enjoyed going out to see live variety acts. As well as singers, comedians and dancers in variety halls, there was the week that the circus came to town. This was a most eagerly anticipated event. People turned out in droves to line the streets as the parade passed by. For the circus proprietors this was a good way in which to advertise the forthcoming attractions. A marching band led the way, followed by camels, dancing dogs, prancing ponies and lumbering elephants. Clowns with large feet and gaily decorated faces sprayed water onto squealing children and everyone oohed and aahed as the acrobats tumbled their way down the street. Men on stilts handed out leaflets, fire-eaters behaved like dragons and pretty trapeze artists and tightrope walkers flashed their eyes and other parts of their anatomies at ogling menfolk. Gardeners followed the elephants with buckets and shovels as they arrived at the top of Regent Street. They anticipated that a bumper crop of rhubarb or special display of roses might result with the assistance of what they collected. When the show under the big top eventually got under way, it was everything the public had expected and the performers were treated to long bursts of tumultuous applause. Billy Smart's Circus was one of the country's best known touring entertainments. Founded by a showman and fairground proprietor, this circus packed in the crowds in the postwar years. At its peak, before animal rights became an issue, the four masted Big Top could hold an audience of over 6,000 who watched spellbound as lion tamers, bareback riders and high wire artists performed remarkable feats. Billy Smart Senior died in 1966, but his sons carried on with a touring show until 1971. Televised performances were still attracting large audiences into the early 1980s.

Left: A fascinating photograph which dates from just before the outbreak of the Second World War. The picture features one of the beautifully decorated function rooms which made up the facilities at the Arcadian Restaurant; note the very ornate plaster-work which characterised the interior of this respected building, along with the pretty leaded windows and delicate electric lights. The venue was the location for this exhibition of various household appliances. Many ordinary people would not have been able to afford the items seen here, though every housewife would no doubt have dreamed of owning a house full of labour-saving devices. To the modern eye the scene looks like an exhibition area in a well-appointed museum, but to the visitors who came here in 1939 this was actually a glimpse into the future.

Bottom left and below: The display in the window of the Yorkshire Electricity Board showroom underlined a housewife's aspirations in 1946. It also demonstrated the way in which a happy, middle class family should live. Mum was the guardian of the house and the organiser of the home. She was in charge of all the cooking, cleaning and caring. Dad was nowhere in sight as,

presumably, he was at work bringing home a salary that provided all the mod cons for the little woman, their well scrubbed child and the family pet. Those women who had endured blisters on the hands as land girls and on their bottoms as ambulance drivers found such advertisements quite patronising. Although some rebelled, most capitulated and women returned to the kitchen sink. Fridges, fires, heaters, washers, cookers and cleaners were domestic aids that would make life around the house so much easier. Even so, they were expensive and still regarded as luxuries. They would not be regarded as essential items for the better part of another two decades.

The showroom on Queens Road promoted the Hoover vacuum cleaner with the slogan, 'springtime is Hoover time'. Even 65 years ago, the name had become synonymous with any type of machine that performed the same function. It was invented in 1908 by JM Spangler, an asthmatic who was plagued by dust every time anyone swept the house. He interested his cousin, Susan Hoover, in developing the cleaner as a commercial enterprise and so the story began in earnest. The most famous of all slogans connected with promoting Hoover, 'it beats, as it sweeps, as it cleans' was first used as far back as 1919.

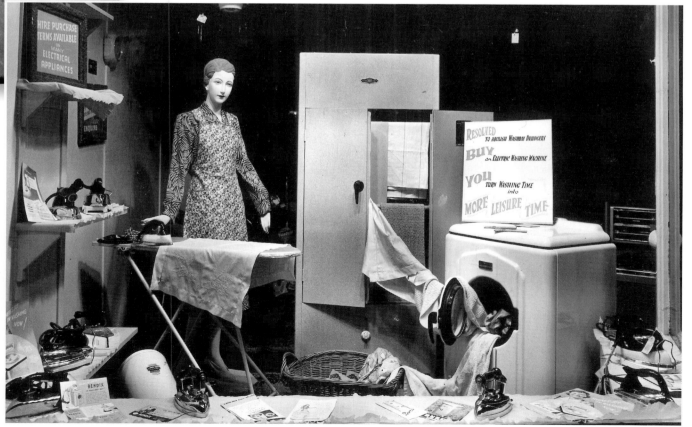

Like many other teams, Barnsley FC has its roots both in soccer and in a church. It was formed in 1887 as Barnsley St Peter's and soon graduated via the Sheffield and District League to the Midland League. Having dropped the St Peter's part of its name, the club joined the Football League's Division Two in 1898. Life was a bit of a struggle for the side as financial backing was limited. Even so, national recognition and a degree of success were just around the corner. The 1909-10 season put Barnsley on the soccer map. An exciting run in the FA Cup saw the Tykes race through the qualifying rounds in great style. Including a couple of replays, seven matches were played in which just one single goal was conceded. Some 16 were scored at the other end as the likes of such top names as Everton and West Bromwich Albion were defeated. The lads were flying high and even used the inspiration of Channel hopping Louis Blériot to celebrate their achievement. Wembley Stadium did not open until 1923, so the final was played at Crystal Palace. Newcastle

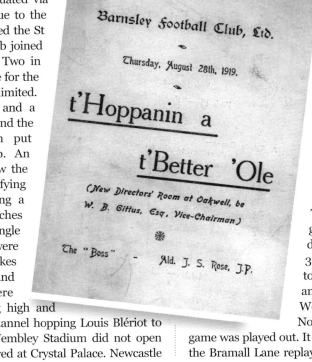

Barnsley Football Club, Ltd.

Thursday, August 28th, 1919.

t'Hoppanin a

t'Better 'Ole

(New Directors' Room at Oakwell, be W. B. Gittus, Esq., Vice-Chairman)

The "Boss" – Ald. J. S. Rose, J.P.

United provided the opposition. The Geordies were the heavy favourites to lift the trophy, having won the League title the previous season and having already played in three of the last five Cup Finals. However, the big boys were shocked when Harry Tufnell, our top FA Cup scorer that season, opened the scoring in the first half. We held on to the lead until near the end, but were denied victory eight minutes from time. In the replay, played at Goodison Park, Newcastle proved too powerful and won 2-0.

Two years later, the boys in red had another strong Cup run. The toughest challenge along the way came from Bradford City, the reigning Cup holders. The quarter final tie was as tough as it gets. The clubs played three goalless draws before Barnsley squeezed through 3-2 after extra time in the third replay. It took ten games to get through five rounds and reach Crystal Palace again where West Bromwich Albion was waiting. Nobody was surprised that yet another 0-0 game was played out. It was the same score after 90 minutes in the Bramall Lane replay, but Tufnell grabbed the winner deep

ON THE WINGS OF FAME TO THE FINAL APRIL 23rd 1910

BARNSLEY'S TEAM

1909-10

into extra time and the Cup was held aloft by skipper Archie Taylor for the one and only time in the history of Barnsley FC. The above photograph was taken at Oakwell and shows the victorious Barnsley side with the F.A.Cup! *The Team that won the Cup that day were; Cooper, Downs, Taylor (Capt), Glendinning, Bratley, Utley, Bartrop, Tufnell, Lillycrop, Travers and Moore.* Harry Tufnell the winning goalscorer is pictured right It was

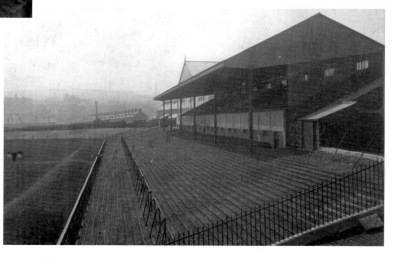

a joyous moment for the team and the town. A landmark occasion celebrated all the way back to Barnsley Town Centre. Despite all their cup exertions the team still managed to finish in a creditable 6th position, 12 points behind promoted pair Derby and Chelsea. Five of the team from the 1910 side played in the final two years on and Barnsley remain only one of a handful of sides with a 50/50 ratio of success in FA Cup finals. The other sides with a win from two appearances are Charlton, Notts County and less well known, Clapham Rovers.

Oakwell Stadium has been the club's home since 1888, though only the West Stand of the original ground remains. Even that has been partly redeveloped to meet the demands of the Taylor Report, when the provision of all seater stadiums was demanded in the 1990s. However, Oakwell had a few facelifts before then, including some remodelling after World War I The programme pictured top left is from a dinner to celebrate the opening of the new Director's Room at Oakwell, 28th August, 1919. The ground capacity presently stands at 23,000, so the record attendance of 40,255 set for an FA Cup tie against Stoke City will never be beaten. Following cup success in 1912, Barnsley spent more than 80 years migrating between the lower divisions before clinching a shock promotion to the Premier League in 1997 under Danny Wilson.

STREETS OF CHANGE

With the Imperial Garage to the right and a view beyond the public conveniences in the foreground, we are looking along Peel Square in the mid 1920s. In the distance, we can see the distinctive building that was instantly recognisable as being part of the Burton tailoring empire. The 'tailor of taste', Montague Burton (1885-1952) was born in Lithuania as Moshe Osinsky. He came to England

in his mid teens and earned his living as a pedlar in Manchester before moving to Chesterfield. Here he sold ready made suits that he bought from a wholesaler. Experiencing some racism that restricted the growth of his business, he opted to change his name, using the nearby town on the Trent as his new surname. He had opened five retail outlets by the start of the First World War, with a manufacturing base in Leeds. The expansion in peacetime was dramatic. By the end of the 1920s he had opened over 400 shops up and down the country. It seemed that a new Burton's store was opening almost on a weekly basis. He was knighted for 'his services to industrial relations' in 1931. The company made a quarter of all British military uniforms during the 1939-45 war and a third of all demobilisation suits issued to ex-servicemen at its end. This gave rise to the phrase 'the full Monty' that was originally applied to getting a complete set of clothes.

Old, worn out housing was still commonplace in 1937. After the 1914-18 war, Lloyd George and his government promised that they would build a new land for the heroes of the trenches and their families. We waited throughout the 1920s, but little materialised. It was only when we were well into the decade that followed that things began to move. By then, another generation had lived through a time when damp ran off the walls, vermin scuttled across the back yards and whole families washed in a tin bath brought in from outside and filled by kettles boiled on a range. The toilet was little better than a privy, located in a flimsy shed across cracked flagstones. Large families were raised in a few cramped

rooms and fathers tried their best to find what work that they could. Their wives had to eke out an existence on the few miserable shillings they had each week that had to pay for everything. They hid from the rentman, pawned their best items and served up what they could. The women worked all hours attempting to keep the place tidy and get the washing done. The houses at 2, 4, 6 and 8 Well Street, alongside the entrance to Court 1, Racecommon Road, that was festooned with washing, existed back to back with 1, 3, 5 and 7 Racecommon Road. Talk about living in each other's pockets; this was almost literally the case. Yet, look at the faces that are turned towards the camera.

Most of them are smiling. They would be smiling all the more when these properties were cleared and they could make their way to new homes on brighter council estates on the other side of town. Pictured above right are tenants in front of rabbit hutches and foul houses adjoining No 7 Court 1, Baker Street, in the 1930s.

The interior of No 9 Court, 4 Blucher Street, shows how poorly some people lived before the last war. The single room was home to this man. It was his living room, kitchen and bedroom combined. This whole area around Wortley Street was part of the compulsory purchase scheme that forced landlords into surrendering their properties into council ownership. The houses could then be demolished and families rehoused in places that had running hot and cold water, inside toilets, gas and electricity. The gang of children seems fascinated by the lens being pointed at them. They would be even more interested in their new homes that had little gardens and where the wallpaper did not have black mould growing on it.

Above and top right: The photographs were taken from approximately the same spot, but about 45 years apart. They show the view along Queen Street from Cheapside in the mid 1930s and again in 1979. Where once there were motorcars we now have pedestrians calmly going about their business, pandering to their particular shopping needs. Some of the shops and their facades have altered little over the years. The original Burton's building on the left is still with us. It had been taken over by the Dolcis shoe shop in the more modern picture and houses the Barnsley Building Society nowadays. Taylor's chemist shop was transformed into Ratner's jewellery business. As a sign of the times, the buildings further down were the Orange phone shop and Noble's Amusements when the second decade of this century began. The distinctively panelled front of the Woolworth store appeared in 1971 and was incorporated two years later with the older version of the five and ten cent store that had opened alongside in 1932. Woolworth stopped trading here in March, 1984. Stores along here now include Dorothy Perkins, Burton's, Evans, Specsavers, Wallis and Optical Express. The mushroomed shaped shelter and benches in the photograph top right were presented by the Rotary Club to mark its golden jubilee in 1973.

Right: The Sheffield Road, Cheapside, area looking up New Street at the site of the soon-to-be-built Alhambra Centre. The near side of the road is being cleared to make way for road widening, Hardy's furnishing shop was situated here between 1965 and 1967 and eventually Dolcis shoes occupied the premises. This was the age of the consumer and goods like washing machines, once regarded as a luxury, were now an essential item in every home. Each house was beginning at this time to acquire its share of other 'labour saving devices' so freeing the housewife - and her husband - from the drudgery of housework and giving more time for leisure pursuits. The advancement of technology, the introduction of colour and the advent of new channels made television viewing a national way of life. Consequently there came the increase in sales of sets and, with the growth of the hire purchase industry and other rental schemes, it allowed firms like DER to prosper.

Above: This picture from the bottom of Market Hill in the 1930s has an ever older feel to it. A number of people are congregating outside the Yorkshire Penny Bank, at the right hand side of the picture. The bank was established in May 1, 1859, by Colonel Edward Akroyd, of Halifax. Based in Leeds, it was originally known as the West Riding Penny Savings Bank. In 1860 it was decided to extend the operation to the other Ridings of Yorkshire and to recognise this the name was changed to the Yorkshire Penny Bank. During the miners' strike of 1984-85 the bank offered miners who were mortgage holders a deferment, allowing them to postpone payments for the duration of the dispute.

is still a major part of town shopping today, though it has been largely housed under the covered centre since the early 1970s. Even so, there is something of a pleasant old world feel about some of the stalls, despite being set in modern surroundings. It is something of an Aladdin's cave where the earnest shopper can discover a stall selling fresh eels and another offering the most obscurely sized nut or bolt imaginable. There is everything from fresh bread and pies to tripe, cow heel and beef dripping. All this is enough to make you think that the clock has been cranked back a few decades. We do miss the open air market as the calls of the traders seemed to resound like nowhere else in town, but such echoes are just a distant memory, though not completely forgotten.

Right: The covered market on Cheapside, seen in 1930, was doing good business. Opposite, Taylor's chemist shop was quite busy. More correctly, the Taylor Drug Company, it was to merge in 1935 with Timothy White's chemist, founded in 1848 in Portsmouth as a general store. Timothy White's and Taylor's did battle royal with Boots for trade on Britain's High Streets until 1968 when the latter emerged triumphant, buying out its rival. The charter to hold a market in Barnsley goes back to the 13th century. It

Above: A later view of Cheapside, in Barnsley. Cheapside is a common street name meaning 'market-place' from the old English 'ceapan', to buy. There was originally no connection to the modern meaning of the word 'cheap' (low price).

Below: An unusual sight in the centre of Barnsley as torrential rain caused widespread flooding. Lightly-dressed shoppers can be seen taking shelter beneath the canvass-topped stalls of the open market as the rain comes down. The background is framed by the white buildings of the Barnsley British Co-operative Society and the skyline is dominated by the sign above Bailey's store proclaiming 'We supply all but the baby.' The large white monument to Barnsley retailing was pulled down in 1960. Among many locals it was known as 'Thorpe's Co-op' because a Mr, W. Thorpe had traded from the location for many years before the retailing giant took it over. The building itself dated from the middle of the last century, and it housed several different departments of the Co-op in its heyday, including Menswear, Drapery, Grocery, Butchering and a Chemists shop.

Pictured above is a 1955 view of Market Hill and next to the entrance to Royal Street Arcade is Guest's cafe a long established family business here. The Arcade was established in 1893 when buildings were demolished to make a passage from Guest's yard to Market Hill. Next door is Boots the Chemist, not a local business, but being here since 1923 has given it some kind of residential status rather like the Midland Bank opposite. The leather goods shop of Spiers was another small firm to establish itself here before it had to give way to the march of commercial progress. Two banks take us to the corner of Eldon Street, one housing the old Yorkshire Penny Bank. Across the road from Guest's to where at one time there used to be a small market, is Cheesman's Printers with its van parked outside and what could be its driver taking the air. A picture to bring back some memories - you can almost smell Guest's roast coffee beans from here. Pictured right is a more modern view from the Town Hall on a chilly day in 1971, we are gazing across Shambles Street and down Market Hill towards the Town Centre. In the distance a crane hovers above Eldon Street, about to do its worst as it did away with the old to bring in the new, in the belief that all change was for the good. What a pity this is not the case and we lost some of our favourite buildings in the name of modernisation. At the time of this picture we can still see the busy outdoor market stalls opposite the distinctive façade of The Halifax Building Society. At the end of Shambles Street we see WH Smith next to Castles and a few doors down from Butterfields & Massies. 'Butterfield's Drapery Market' is still the inscription over the door, despite its closure in 1975. The store was run by successive generations of families, starting in the 1930s. The more eagle-eyed reader will have noticed that Marks & Spencer have moved in on the later picture, at the bottom of Market Hill, next to Goodsons.

Right: Traffic is making very slow headway on the part of Sheffield Road where it drops down from below Park Road into Cheapside. The re-surfacing work collects its fair share of interested possibly critical spectators and shoppers' progress is being impeded by it all. The road contained some of the more celebrated shopping names in Barnsley like Horsfields at nos 59 to 63, on the right below the Odeon. This shop, like the others, closed in 1971. Its windows were a mini department store of its own as it could in one cramped space display all manner of boots and shoes, quilts, watches and suits among other things as well as being, like Harrals on the same road, a pawnbroker. There was the grocery department of the Co-op here, Cantor's furniture store across the road from the Odeon, which closed in 1969, Palmer's drapers shop and next door at 154 its grocers shop. Like the market, you could buy anything on this street from sewing machines to toys to motor cycles; no wonder Bovril was advertised so prominently, a shopper would need it after a trip here to all those shops.

Top right: A new decade had just dawned as we look along Church Street at lunch time on 11 January, 1950. Of course, the traffic over 60 years ago was light by modern standards. The colours and styling of the vehicles' coachwork reflected the times. They were uniformly dark and utilitarian. There we were, at the start of the second half of the 20th century, but with little to brighten our days. The war was over, but we were still paying for it. Rebuilding bomb damaged towns and cities was horrendously expensive and we were in debt to the Americans to such an extent that it would take until the next century for the slate to be cleared. In the meantime, life in Barnsley continued sedately enough. Students enrolled for the new term at the College of Technology, seen on the left, while middle class housewives popped into Barclays Bank to draw out a couple of pounds that would be enough to purchase a few days' supplies before they needed to come into town once more.

Right: Shopping in the early 1920s was little different from the same activity conducted over the following decades. It was just that little bit more relaxed after the Great War as the crowds were smaller and the opportunities to browse and window shop all the greater. Note the couple on the left. They are people for whom the modern term 'fashion statement' could have been invented. He is nattily attired in a smart suit and stylish hat. His companion has the period cloche hat prettily perched on her attractive head, while her skirt length is of the modern style. Cut just below the knee, it is many inches higher than she would have dared in Edwardian times. Then, it was all about full length dresses and high necked blouses. The war put paid to all that sort of encumbrance. Women played a major role in keeping the country running while the menfolk were at the front. There was no time for the niceties of polite dress and women dressed as the job demanded. They would not surrender all freedom in peacetime and that manifested itself in many ways. Emancipation was not just about the vote, but also about freedom to choose what to wear and how to behave. Even so, there were some old fashioned niceties that could be observed. As they shopped on Church Street, the man still walked next to the road to protect his loved one from the traffic. She enjoyed this little piece of chivalry, despite her independent spirit.

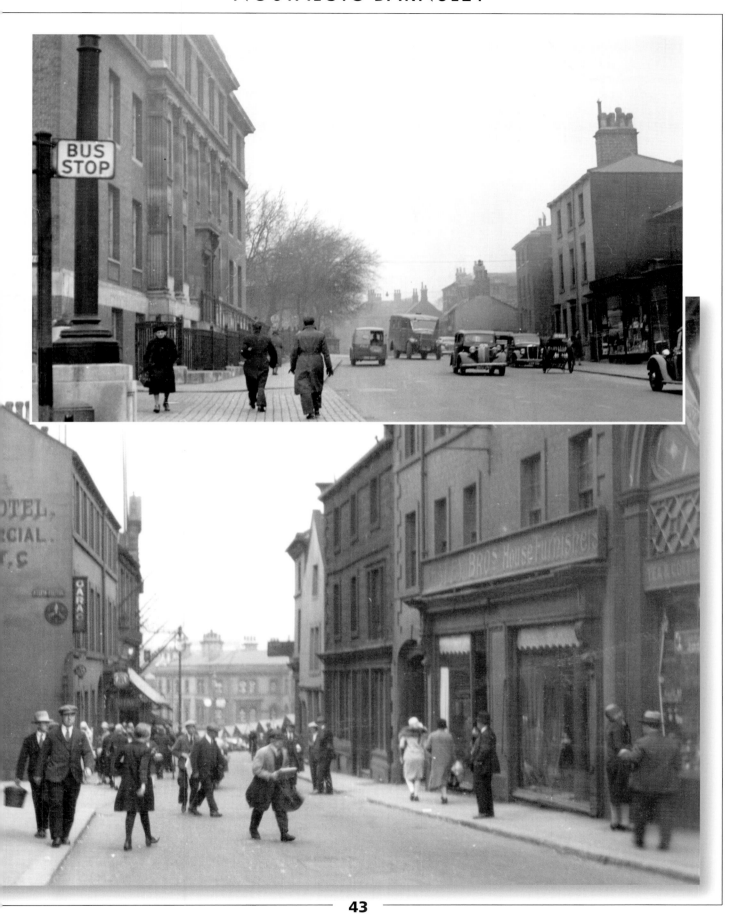

Below: The view that says 'This is Barnsley'. The Town Hall and the Technical and Mining College stand in line at the top of the hill. An occasional visitor to any town takes away usually one memory of it. In the case of Barnsley it is the Town Hall. This photograph was taken possibly in the late 1950s when there is life about Market Hill, not, as it sometimes appears today, of just traffic worming its way toward Shambles Street. The market stalls, the vans, the parked cars and the crowds they attracted were central to the life of the street and the businesses like Harts, Woodhouse Currys, the Midland Bank, Zuckers and Goodworths, having been there for some time, give it its own kind of permanence. The building at the corner of Market Hill and Shambles Street was once the site of the Corn Exchange which burnt down in 1927. The policeman overseeing the zebra crossing would be a familiar figure with his own kind of authority here long before traffic wardens and pelican crossings, although there is someone sneaking across the road behind his back.

Top right: Could this be a scene from Quadrophenia, the 1979 British film loosely based around the rock opera of the same name by The Who? Perhaps not, the date of the picture and the scooters may not give the game away, however most Barnsley folk would recognise this is Queen Street and not an area in Shepherd's Bush, West London, where most of the filming took place. Some familiar hostelries can be seen in the background, including the Market Inn and Wire Trellis Hotel. These scooter enthusiasts are not out looking for a confrontation with a gang of 'Rockers', they are in fact part of the Barnsley Vespa Club, co-

opted into helping promote a new film release at the Barnsley Gaumont Cinema. The film in question was, 'No My Darling Daughter' a 1961 British comedy featuring Sir Michael Redgrave and Juliet Mills. Redgrave had been knighted two years earlier in 1959. The scooter became an integral part of British youth culture in the 1960s as a favourite mode of transport of the fashion-conscious Modernists, or better known 'Mods'. The fully restored Lambretta Li 150 ridden by Phil Daniels in Quadrophenia, with the original film number plate KRU 251F, was sold at Bonhams auction house for £36,000 in November, 2008.

Bottom right: Looking down the eastern approach along Sheffield Road towards the town centre, this 1956 view takes in the Alhambra Theatre. It opened in 1915 with a concert given by Countess Fitzwilliam. The theatre was designed by PA Hinchcliff and catered for an audience of 2,362 in the stalls and on three separate balconies. The capacity was reduced to just over 2,000 in 1939 when the uppermost level was closed. It was built as a variety palace, but at a time when tastes were changing. It lasted a mere 10 years as a live theatre before closing in June, 1925, for refitting as a cinema. 'Koenigsmark' was the first film to be

shown. It was an adventure story based on a French novel written in 1918. Sound was introduced in 1930 and the golden age of cinemagoing at the Alhambra was ushered in. It was grand place for an evening on the town. The stone façade, its columns and the curved pediment above made it a handsome sight. In 1938, Oscar Deutsch took it into his burgeoning chain of Odeon cinemas, but retained the original name that was carved in the stonework outside. 'The Entertainer', starring Laurence Olivier, was the last film shown here before its closure in 1960. It stood empty for two years before becoming a bingo hall. The building was knocked down in 1982 and the Alhambra Shopping Centre took its place.

At the time this expansive panoramic view was being taken, changes to this part of the town were afoot. The scaffolding in the bottom left corner and the massive tower crane in the background tell us something about the magnitude of these changes. Within two years of this shot the Cross Keys Hotel, which had stood on the site since the time of Queen Victoria, had been demolished. The scene is a busy market day with a policeman on crossing duties. It is probably his mini van that is parked outside Paige's fashion shop. As a shopping and commercial centre, Barnsley has always served a wide surrounding area and Barnsley's market has a long history of importance as the commercial and social heart of the town. Barnsley market has been in its time the largest open-air market in the north of England and has attracted people in their

thousands every Wednesday, Friday and Saturday. The 1948 Barnsley Official Handbook described the market as consisting of "300 and 400 canvas-covered stalls, covering an area of between three and four acres". At this time, it was divided into six separate markets: May Day Green, Lower May Day Green, Market Hill, Kendray, Queen's and New Market. Being recognised as one of the largest and best markets for business in the country, stallholders came every week from all over the UK. A shopping centre naturally developed around the site of the historic market. The character of the market has changed in modern times. A new market complex was constructed in 1974 when the town centre shopping centre was redeveloped and there have been no stalls on Market Hill for many years.

Premier Foods
Creating Great Food and Brands Loved By All

Today Premier Food's site at Fish Dam Lane in Carlton, in Barnsley, is one of the area's largest employers. There can be few people in Britain who have not sampled its products, not least the millions of mince pies produced each Christmas.

In the early 1970s when the Carlton site was still a disused pithead, top level discussions at Lyons Bakery's head office confirmed that Cadby Hall in London, its traditional home, and satellite bakeries elsewhere, were no longer suitable. They would not be able to cope with the manufacturing and distribution needs of the 1980s, 1990s and beyond.

The decision was made to build the biggest and most modern bakery in the whole of Europe, if not the whole world. Finding a suitable site for a bakery of the size envisaged was a problem in itself. The ideal location had to be central to the motorway network, allowing production to get into the distribution system quickly.

Importantly, too, a labour force was needed of the quality and quantity that would carry out the work to the standards demanded.

Ideally any site chosen should also be one which attracted Government support in the form of development grants.

Support

A number of areas throughout the UK were looked at over a period of two years and one by one rejected as unsuitable. In the end Carlton was identified by the Company as the preferred location and, to invite the support of local officials and those concerned in industry, a reception was held at Barnsley Town Hall.

The site of the new factory was listed in the Domesday Book. By the 19th century it formed part of the estates of the first Baron Wharncliffe.

In 1872 the third Baron Wharncliffe was instrumental in developing mine workings on 1,300 acres around Carlton village. Sinking shafts began there in August 1874, and eventually five in total would be sunk – two at the far end of the factory site.

Amongst the problems encountered was that of dealing with three quarters of a million gallons of water each from the water bearing rock strata.

When the mine was first developed the transport of goods and raw materials was

Top: *An early view of the Carlton site.*
Left: *The energy centre in the 1970s.*
Above: *The site had provided work for the Barnsley mining community.*

were a priority to eliminate the heat and humidity that had until then created difficult conditions for people working in the industry.

The previously wide geographical spread of the Company's factories in various places and of various sizes and ages, with old and inflexible plant, had led to inefficiencies that were to be remedied with the building of the bakery at Carlton.

Management control and communications needed to be streamlined. There was a pressing need to introduce new techniques for processing and handling and to introduce new plant for improved production in far less time and at far less cost.

by rail and water, with the Barnsley Canal cutting across the present bakery site.

Mining of course was always a dangerous business. Fatalities and injuries were never uncommon. In the early hours of Saturday 8th August 1936 however a huge underground explosion had catastrophic results. All the miners working in the vicinity were lost. The final toll was 58 dead, with many Carlton families losing close relatives and loved ones.

At its peak the mine had a yearly output of nearly half a million tons of coal, but as reserves were exhausted output dwindled. In 1970 the last shaft entrance was filled in and the mine closed.

At Cadby Hall for instance, raw materials had to be lifted through six floors to start the manufacturing process. Each production plant had its various processing operations on several floors, creating handling difficulties at the interchanges, and products had to follow a tortuous route to reach the point of packing and marshalling for despatch. At Carlton all this would be changed.

Above: A laboratory in 1975. Below: Tony Blackburn signs autographs for staff on his visit to Premier Foods in 1979.

On 12th July 1972 the old pithead's chimney stack was razed to the ground, signaling the start of demolition work. To ensure that the sub-soil on the 62-acre site would support the proposed new factory site surveys and borings were carried out. There had to be certainty that the walls would not crack nor the buildings subside as a result of the previous mine workings.

In November 1972 work began on creating the site levels that would allow the structure of the bakery to be stepped into the gently rising land.

Priority

Flexibility and space were needed to allow for plant changes, and facilities of the very highest order were to be provided for personnel. Comfortable working conditions

Over the years, the Company had built up a store of technical and managerial information that was irreplaceable. It was important therefore that as many managers, supervisors and key personnel as possible should be persuaded to come to Carlton from the existing factories.

Recruitment

Existing staff would form a solid foundation of experience, to which could be added new staff recruited locally, in what would be the Company's biggest ever recruitment campaign.

A relocation unit was established to ensure that current staff could make the transfer to Carlton with minimum disruption to their private lives. Guided weekend tours of the area gave them a good idea of what sort of life they could expect. The local council made housing available, and house purchase prices were so favourable that many were able to buy their own homes for the first time in their lives.

January 1973 saw work begin on laying drains and foundations. Floor space of the new factory would occupy more than seven acres. It had been agreed with the local authority that the enormous colliery slagheap that had dominated the site for so

many years would be landscaped to improve the immediate locality.

Amazingly as it now seems the slag was found to be still hot, smouldering and almost volcanic.

Hygiene

The new bakery was built to meet new standards of hygiene then unique in the industry. There were to be no opening windows in the production building and no open access which might allow the ingress of dirt, pests or other contaminants. The environment was to be controlled in both temperature and

*Top: The Mayors parade float in the late 1970's. Money was raised by the Lyons bakery to purchase a minibus for the Variety Club of Great Britain. **Above left:** Kim Richards is crowned Miss Lyons at one of Lyons Bakery Gala's in the late 1970's **Below:** Employees at the Town Hall for a presentation for Basic Hygiene Awards in the mid-1980s.*

humidity, with filtered air. Halls throughout the building were to be tiled in ceramic in the production and packaging areas, and in thermoplastic in 'goods inward' and despatch areas. They were easy on the eye, durable, and of course non-slip.

All ceilings were to be suspended below the service pipe ducts to prevent accumulation of dust and dirt. Side walls were to be tiled and curved to eliminate 'dirt track' corners and prevent trucks from damaging the walls. Where possible, and economically viable, painted surfaces were to be avoided: stainless steel and coated materials were used instead. Cleanliness and hygiene were so vital to the overall concept that no reasonable expense was spared in securing the very best materials.

Materials

A system was designed to eliminate the heavy humping of materials that had previously been necessary. Materials were now to be delivered to the site in road tankers and stored in a large silo. They were to be weighed and measured centrally to the individual mixers, with the whole operation carried out by computer.

Allied to this use of the latest technology, and

during the design stage of production plants, consideration was given to the use of existing machines wherever possible. A typical example of this policy was the Harvest Pie machinery which was to be transferred from Cadby Hall to Carlton.

At Cadby Hall dismantling the machines ready for the 200-mile journey to Yorkshire was a daunting task even for the experts. But once they arrived at Carlton, a completely different set of conditions faced the contractors: a partly finished building, unfinished roads and a great deal of mud. Engineers now had to unload and haul each machine section into place - just the start of a formidable task of joining the parts together, rewiring and connecting power, carrying out an overhauling programme and turning the assembled components into two machines capable of turning out 14,000 Popular Pies an hour.

The first puff of smoke from the plant's chimney in October 1974 meant that the first boiler was fired. Three identical ones would be used to provide low pressure steam for the air conditioning system and for all the process and domestic hot water. Happily, enquiries revealed that locally mined coal would be a secure and economical fuel for the factory's purposes in the immediate future. Uncertainties over the supply of natural gas, and the high cost of piping the supply to the site, however led to the choice of liquefied petroleum gas for the cake ovens.

One interesting feature was an ornamental pond intended to be both an integral part of the landscape, and to provide an emergency supply of water. That pond later had to be filled in because it was impossible to prevent local children from using it as a swimming pool. There was also a danger that, because of the size of the exit pipe, children could have been sucked into it.

By summer 1974 acres of cloying mud had been tamed, roads had been laid and a large parking area completed; some areas of the administration block were ready too. The bakery had already

*Top: A photo from 2000, of staff who were with the Company right from the start. **Left:** HRH The Princess Royal pays a visit to the factory in 1992. On her visit she received a cheque for £30,000 from Lyons Bakeries (UK) Ltd for Save The Children Fund. **Above:** The world's first fully-automated Battenberg plant at Carlton in 1987.*

Legend has it that the first Battenberg cake was made on the whim of a German princess who admired the chequered pattern on a castle's marble floor. Carlton's Battenberg plant went on line in 1976 and very soon was producing enough cake to keep not only a princess happy, but an entire nation. (In 2010 the plant would aim for the Guinness Book of Records with a Battenberg 21.5 metres long!)

By 1976 the bakery had recruited its 1,000th employee and had become one of the most important businesses in the area.

In 2006 Manor Bakeries decided to invest tens of millions in the expansion of its cake manufacturing operations; over the following three years it would create an additional 300 jobs in Barnsley.

The most exciting change to date was when the site became part of Premier Foods in 2007. The Premier Foods portfolio contains category leading brands in nearly every sector of food manufacture so they were a

come a long way since the design team first arrived on site, and staff, many of them recruited locally, had worked in portakabins around the site, There had been no sign then of the familiar caps and overall uniforms so essential in a food production factory, Thick, warm clothing, safety helmets and wellington boots were the order of the day for the early pioneers.

Now, staff such as recruitment personnel, were installed in spacious, well-appointed open plan offices. The restaurant was commissioned, with a range of hot meals and a different menu each day. In the bakery itself, the best possible conditions had been created for the staff: attractive changing rooms with airing lockers to allow damp outdoor clothing to dry, and sufficient showers to cope with rush periods. The medical department was completed and ready to deal with both routine health checks and illness at work at any time. A range of uniforms was specially chosen to identify and suit the various jobs and functions, some of which would be done by women for the very first time. Female staff showed a splendid aptitude for unfamiliar new roles such as forklift truck driving, oven minding and machine work, all previously done almost exclusively by men.

Top left: A very proud Philip Buckley receives the prestigious Investor In People Award on behalf of the Company from Frank Carter, Chairman of the Barnsley Doncaster Training & Enterprise Council. Above: The 21.5 metres long Battenberg, waiting for a Guinness World Record! Right and below: Views inside the plant.

Monday 1st April 1975 was D-Day - the deadline for the start of production of the very first product, Harvest Pie. Managers and staff had to work Good Friday, Saturday, Sunday and Easter Monday to meet the deadline, but meet it they did. The Cup Cake Plant followed, and many others over the next two years. The market began to change thereafter and a number of new products were launched over the next five years or so.

The bakery at Carlton was by then already a local landmark surrounded by the space and greenery of a freshly created development, not very far from the very centre of Britain.

perfect match for the much celebrated brands that the site produced.

The new enlarged group leapfroged Mars, Nestlé and Northern Foods to become the country's number one food producer with sales of £2.6bn - more than 90 per cent of which will be within the UK.

In 2008 a new Learning Centre was opened providing a unique training opportunity for staff and the Company by working in partnership.

Today, with its fortieth anniversary in sight, the bakery at Carlton has become merged with the landscape. A new generation of staff has grown up in the locality never knowing anything else. Fewer and fewer recall the pits which previously occupied the area. Yet one important relic does survive from the mining era: those who worked in the coal industry and their families were famous for their profound sense of community spirit. Today that spirit continues at Carlton: those who work there have raised thousands upon thousands of pounds for charities, including Cancer Research UK, Barnsley Hospice, Weston Park Hospital, MacMillan Nurses and The Eve Appeal (Ovarian Cancer).

The combination of amazing brands and great people truly make our site an incredible place to come to work every day.

*Top: A bird's eye view inside the factory. **Centre:** Just two examples of the various fund-raising activities arranged by Premier Foods. **Below:** An aerial view of Premier Foods' Carlton site in 2010.*

EVENTS & OCCASIONS

Below: Employers often needed to provide their workforce with accommodation, the quality of which varied greatly. Earl Fitzwilliam provided some of the best contemporary housing for his workers in the model community of Elsecar. George Utley, the Barnsley soccer player who won an England cap in 1913, was born on Reform Row in 1887. That international game against Ireland occurred a year after the visit of King George V and Queen Mary. The royal couple stopped off at Elsecar Colliery during their time in the West Riding. Reform Row was brightly decorated in their honour as the route took them through the village. Locals had a chance to see the monarch and his consort in the flesh and this was not an opportunity to be missed, so they came out of their homes all ready to wave and cheer. Some of the flags, streamers and bunting had been used the previous

year when the Coronation took place. Elsecar Heritage Centre, situated near here on Wath Road, is located within the former Earl Fitzwilliam ironworks and colliery workshops. The restored historical buildings make it a living museum and the Centre is home to the only Newcomen beam engine that has remained in its original location.

Above: The Amalgamated Society of Railway Servants was founded in 1872. It was the forerunner of the National Union of Railwaymen that was established in 1913 when several societies, unions and organisations combined under one banner. The Cudworth section marched along Barnsley Road in 1909 in support of the Orphans' Fund. Workers not only established trusts and even homes for children who had lost their parents, but provided modest pensions and payments to families who had fallen on hard times. The charitable fund depended upon donations from both its workforce and from the general public. A procession such as this helped keep the plight of those who were suffering deprivation in the public gaze. These were times when government aid for the needy was minimal. Although some orphanages were established, they did not generally accept youngsters under the age of six. However, some of the children were not true orphans, but had mothers who simply had insufficient funds to feed and clothe them. That was the harsh reality of life in Victorian and Edwardian times.

Above: The female dignitaries sat sedately on their benches as the regimental band headed towards them at the bottom of Market Hill on 12 July, 1912. The rousing marches being played heralded the arrival of King George V and Queen Mary as they made their way into the town centre as part of their official visit to Barnsley. Bunting was stretched across the road and banners were hung from windows and displayed on walls with messages of support and affection for them both. He was nearly 45 when he succeeded his father, Edward VII, in 1910. As a child, he had not been groomed for kingship. His elder brother, Albert, was the second in line to the throne, after their father. Things changed dramatically in 1891 when Albert died of pneumonia.

He had been engaged to Princess Mary of Teck, but George was encouraged to propose to her as she was seen as a suitable candidate for the role of future Queen. Despite such a seemingly loveless start, the couple became devoted to one another. King George is remembered in royal circles for breaking the ties with

Germany. When war broke out in 1914, he relinquished all titular connection with that country. He issued a royal proclamation in 1917, changing the name of the Royal House from Saxe-Coburg-Gotha to Windsor.

Bottom left: During their tour of the West Riding, King George V and Queen Mary took time out to call in on the residents of Penistone. In July, 1912, despite there being a few showers to dampen the mood, most spectators were as pleased as Punch to welcome their honoured guests. Not everybody was a monarchist, though. Many of the working classes were unhappy with their lot. The growing power of trades unions meant that there was more open conflict with the establishment and some saw the King and Queen as the personification of unearned privilege. Quite a few of the titled heads of Europe slept uneasily in their beds. The trio of cousins, George of England, Wilhelm of Germany and Nicholas of Russia, would soon find their positions under threat. In 1918, Nicholas would be murdered after a revolution and Wilhelm abdicate and flee after a mutiny of his armed forces. George held on to his throne partly because of his sympathy for striking workers in 1926 when he told critics who called them revolutionaries, 'Well, try living on their wages'.

Above: Hiram Codd was an English engineer. In 1872, he patented a bottle filled under gas pressure which pushed a marble against a rubber washer in the neck, creating a perfect seal. The globe stoppered bottle helped make his fortune. In September 1873, he met Ben Rylands and by 1877 they formed a partnership and started the Hope Glass Works in Barnsley. The expression 'codswallop' has its origins in the fizzy mineral water contained in their bottles that real beer drinkers despised. The businessmen remained partners until Ben's death in 1881. The latter's son, Dan, inherited Ben's holding, but bought out Codd in 1884. When King George V and Queen Mary visited Rylands' Glass Works they were shown the process of bottle manufacture, including a special one that Dan Rylands himself invented. The 'anti-theft' bottle was an aqua bottle whose top or lip was made of a coloured glass to identify one particular company. Collectors of such items scramble over one another to acquire an example. In this picture the king is looking quizical as the glassmaking operation was described to him. The Queen was less interested, but diplomatically kept her counsel.

Above: For over 40 years, the Ecclesfield Hospital Parade was one of the highlights of the local recreational calendar. People would don fancy dress or put on their best bib and tucker. Brightly decorated floats, created from carts or, in later years, lorry backs adorned the procession through the town that lies a few miles north of Sheffield. A band would play and there would be sports on the field and a fairground for the children to enjoy. Any profits from the events went into a central fund to which spectators also contributed with donations dropped into buckets and collecting boxes rattled in front of them. This was 1911, a generation and more before the coming of the National Health Service. Hospitals relied on contributions from bequests, donations and charity to help make ends meet. Without such fund raising, medical care would only have been provided for the wealthy and the poor left to their own devices. The Ecclesfield Hospital Parade was first held in the 1890s and was repeated annually on the third Saturday after Whitsuntide. Different parishes, neighbourhoods, organisations and businesses all provided floats and there was a keen but friendly rivalry between the various factions. Getting an award for the best dressed float was quite an honour. The procession began in Station Road, where the judging took place. Then, the mammoth journey began, running via Grenoside to Wadsley Bridge, past Sheffield

Infirmary and through to Moorfoot. The return journey would not be completed until about 8pm, when a feast was held by the Bull Inn. One jolly feature of the parade was a team of 'Plough Bullocks'. A plough was placed on the back of a cart and pulled by ploughman dressed in old fashioned agricultural smocks. To complete the silliness, their faces were blacked and their heads adorned with top hats. Their leader whipped them with a device made from pigs' bladders tied to a stick. Needless to say, the ploughmen were well 'watered' along the way with beer supped from galvanised buckets. The last parade was held in 1936 and another little piece of tradition disappeared.

Left: The Barnsley Hospital Aviation Meeting took place in 1913 and featured a Blériot monoplane as one of its main attractions. This early flying machine, one of the first to have just one pair of wings, was manufactured by the company belonging to the aviator, inventor and engineer who came to the notice of the British public in 1909. Louis was the first man to fly the English Channel when he beat off several rivals to win the £1,000 prize on offer from the Daily Mail.

His success as a pilot provided a valuable advertising tool and his company built more than 800 aeroplanes over the next five years. He established flying schools at Brooklands and Hendon and, after World War I, founded a very successful company that produced commercial aircraft. He continued to be involved with the industry up to his death in 1936. The crowd that came to watch Mr BC Mucks fly one of Blériot's planes was said to number 10,000, such was the interest in this marvellous piece of technology. For many, it was their first opportunity to witness such a wonderful event as the monoplane made five flights over the showground.

Above: Clearly a great deal of thought, effort and imagination has gone into this fancy dress parade on Haigh Lane, Hoylandswaine. It is thought that the parade may have been linked to Peace Day celebrations to mark the end of World War One. It is still often forgotten that the war did not officially end on 11 November, 1918, as the treaty negotiations at Versailles continued long into the following year. In Britain the Peace Committee met for the first time in May, 1919. Lord Curzon, the Foreign Secretary, who loved pomp and ceremony, outlined a celebration running over four days, including a Victory March through London, a day of Thanksgiving services, a river pageant, and a day of popular festivities. Lloyd George favoured something simpler, but the the rest of the Cabinet supported Curzon. In any event the signing of peace at the end of June meant that arrangements had to be hastily arranged and the celebration was fixed for 19 July, 1919.

Above: When Johnny comes marching home again, hurrah, hurrah. The town celebrated the return of the Barnsley Battalions on 29 May, 1919. It was a proud day, yet a sad one, too. So many fine men would not be making that march this day or any other. The grateful public turned out in their thousands to salute these brave chaps in scenes that were repeated all over the nation. Drums beat a mournful tattoo and buglers played the Last Post with as much solemnity as they could muster. The first official Remembrance Day was dedicated by King George V on 7 November, 1919, and is now recalled at the 11th hour on the 11th day of that month each year. Parades and services are usually held on the second Sunday of November. When the troops went off to the front in the late summer of 1914 they were taking part in what was originally known as the European War. It was only after it ended that reference to 'the Great War' was made. Sadly, we had to call it 'World War I' from the mid 1940s onwards.

Top right (two pictures): David Lloyd George was one of the most charismatic political figures of the early 20th century. As the only British Prime Minister who had English as his second language, he is something of a quiz question in a game of Trivial Pursuits. Born in Manchester in 1863, as a baby he moved with his Welsh parents to Pembrokeshire. His father died a year later and the family moved to North Wales to live with David's uncle, a staunch Liberal and an influential figure in the boy's upbringing. Lloyd George studied law but was always keenly interested in politics. He became a Member of Parliament in 1890. As a vehement opponent of the Boer War, his name was soon known to the public. In 1906 he became a member of the Cabinet as President of the Board of Trade, rising to the influential position of Chancellor of the Exchequer two years later. He was keen on social reform and championed the introduction of the first pension and sickness benefits that we now take for granted. Getting sick pay became known as 'going on the Lloyd George'. He was elevated to the prime ministerial role in 1916 and held this office for six years. His attendance, accompanied by his wife, Margaret, at this wedding at All Saints, Darton's parish church on 27 August, marked the occasion as one of the society events of 1921. Sir William Sutherland and Miss Annie Christine Fountain were married in a ceremony that was attended by local and national dignantries, as well as friends and family members. As a member of parliament, Sir William Sutherland rose throught the ranks to become David Lloyd George's Private Secretary. David Lloyd George remained a force in politics for another 20 years, but never regained high office after leaving Downing Street. He was created a peer in 1945, but died before taking up his seat in the House of Lords.

Below: Situated on the B6411 road, Great Houghton is a small village of about 2,000 inhabitants to the west of Thurnscoe. The reason for this street party is unknown, but it is thought to have taken place around 1920.

Above: Members of the Junior Naturalists' Association were all spruced up and ready to attend church on this day in 1961. The youngsters, guided by a group of willing adult helpers and instructors, were taking part in a 'Know Your Countryside' course that helped them better understand the rural environment of the spot where they had come for a short residential stay. Although the building has not been identified, there are many centres up and down the country, such as former village schools, youth hostels and outdoor pursuit bases that cater for such interests. Of course, these young people had to smile weakly when their friends made jokes about them removing their clothes. 'Ha-ha, very funny,' they said for the umpteenth time that their pals deliberately confused naturalist with naturist. While not many of the children contemplated a career in ecology or environmental matters, nearly all continued to have a healthy interest in the outdoors. You can see them now as members of ramblers' clubs, out for a walk every weekend, rucksacks on their backs, maps in plastic cases around their necks and Leki sticks held firmly in their grasp.

Below: Joy Week ran from July 4 to 11 in 1936. Despite not having a lot about which to be joyous, given the state of the national economy, Barnsley folk let their hair down and enjoyed seven days of fun and frolics. Never mind that conditions were so bad and work so scarce that marchers from Jarrow would descend upon London later that year, we were going to make the most of what we had. The procession had reached Town End. The film being shown at the cinema this week was a rather obvious and silly comedy about a lord who is forced by circumstance to take a job as a footman. 'Come out of the Pantry' had the advantage of starring two of the biggest box office names of the era. Fay Wray had already come to international prominence as the girl in the gorilla's clutches in the 1933 movie 'King Kong'. The part was originally meant for Jean Harlow, but she was under exclusive contract to another company. Wray went on to appear in a number of other horror films, earning the nickname of 'scream queen'. However, here she was in a much lighter role, playing opposite Jack Buchanan. He was an elegant Scotsman who was both an actor and accomplished singer. The Ivor Novello composition 'And her mother came too' became one of his smash hit songs.

Right: Prince Albert, the Duke of York, was quite content with his niche in the royal family. So was his wife, the former Elizabeth Bowes-Lyons. However, that all changed in 1936 when his brother, Edward VIII, abdicated. The shy, stammering heir to the throne was thrust into the public eye in a way that he could ever have envisaged. However, he had a strong, protective woman at his side. She often took centre stage as she sought to shield his weaknesses from scrutiny. We became used to see her hogging the limelight, not out of arrogance but from a sense of duty in protecting the man who she loved. He was happy to play second fiddle whenever he could. Here, they stood at the rear of Wesley Street, looking towards Pontefract Road. The photograph, taken by an off duty policeman, dates from 1944. Seen here on a royal visit to Barnsley in 1944, Queen Elizabeth the Queen Mother looks radiant and is smiling like she has just shared a joke with the Mayor. The Lady Mayoress on the other hand is 'not amused'.

Below: A blue plaque to one of the town's best known sons can be found on the wall at the Cooper Art Gallery, the former Holgate Grammar School, on Church Street. Joseph Locke (1805-60) was educated there, though he was born in Attercliffe, Sheffield. The family moved to Barnsley when he was just five years of age. After failing to apply himself to any particular profession, he was apprenticed to George Stephenson in 1823 and worked on the Stockton-Darlington and Liverpool-Manchester railways. His skill saw him become the chief engineer for the Grand Junction Railway and he was heavily involved in the town planning of Crewe. He also designed the railway line from Manchester to Sheffield that included the three mile Woodhead Tunnel. Locke worked with distinction on the Continent and was decorated with the Legion of Honour by Napoleon III for the quality of his

work. He became president of the Institute of Civil Engineers in 1857. By then, he had served Honiton as its MP for eight years and would continue to do so until his death from complications with appendicitis. Although responsible for designing some remarkable bridges, including the dramatic 20-arch Dutton Viaduct over the River Weaver, in Cheshire, his greatest legacy is the modern day West Coast main line. This was formed by joining the Caledonian, Lancaster and Carlisle and Grand Junction railways to Robert Stephenson's London and Birmingham Railway. In 1834, he married Phoebe McCreery. In 1862, she presented Locke Park to the public in his memory and a statue to him was erected there in 1866. This was sculpted by the exotically named Baron Carlo Marochetti of Vaux. The original site was created on 17 acres of land known as High Stile Field and initially named People's Park. Its design cleverly incorporated an existing quarry. Phoebe's sister, Sarah, more than doubled the area of the park when she donated a further 21 acres of land in 1874. The folly or memorial tower was added in 1877 in memory of Phoebe. It affords a fine view across the town and the Worsbrough Valley. The handsome gardens were laid out by William Barron and Son, from Derbyshire. A bandstand was added in 1908.

The War Memorial Sub-Committee of Barnsley Town Council selected the site in Church Street, raised the money by public subscription and organised the erection of the monument. It was unveiled on Sunday, 11 October, 1925, by General Sir Charles Harington. This picture is likely to have been taken during the dedication ceremony as thousands of local folk look on. The stone cenotaph has a 2.4m high bronze statue on top which shows a helmeted infantryman in a greatcoat, his rifle grounded, standing at ease. The facade facing Church Street has a carved stone wreath above the main inscription. On the rear facade, facing the Town Hall, is a panel showing the winged female figure of Victory. She holds a standard, topped by a wreath, in her left hand and a grounded shield in her right.

Below: Any visit from a member of the Royal Family is very welcome, but one from the monarch and her consort is doubly so. On 27 October, 1954, Queen Elizabeth II and Prince Philip came to town on a formal civic visit. The couple were greeted warmly by both the local dignitaries and the general public. Thousands lined the route into town from the station where they had arrived in the royal train. As the motorcade took them into the centre, the cheering could be heard from a long way off. Those were the days when we came out onto the streets just to get a glimpse of people who we only really saw on Pathé newsreels at the cinema or in stills in the newspaper. Of course, the public's regard for the Windsors was much higher in those days than it is now. The boy being presented to the Queen must have regarded this day as one of the highlights of his short life. Queen Elizabeth was still a relatively young woman, not yet out of her 20s.

Right: The headline stated 'Barnsley rolls out the carpet for the royal couple' and the less formal aspects of current royal visits were demonstrated in Her Majesty the Queen's visit with Prince Phillip to Barnsley in July, 1975. Twenty thousand people had gathered in sweltering heat to see their majesties, their first visit here for 21 years. The ceremonial was still evident as the pair were greeted by the Mayor, Councillor Harold Brain, civic officials and County Council officers at the new County Offices. Music was provided by the Grimethorpe Colliery Band and bouquets were presented by Gillian Brain and Anne Burkenshaw. The more informal aspects of their fifty-five minute stay in the town occured with the walk from the new County Offices to the equally new market complex when they met members of the vast crowd including several senior citizens and four lucky schoolboys from Royston. Paul Todd, Peter Green, Wayne Derby and Geoffrey Miller.

Above and right: On 6 May, 1960, Princess Margaret was married. She, it appeared, had found true love once again. Britain had followed the life of this royal with keen interest. Her elder sister was our Queen, but Margaret Rose was seldom out of the headlines. Born in 1930, she was a glamorous figure on the social circuit in the late 1940s and early 1950s. Often featuring in gossip columns, her involvement with her father's equerry, the former Group Captain Peter Townsend, became a matter of national interest. He was a divorcee and, because of this, regarded as an improper suitor for a person then third in line to the throne. After much heart searching and painful consideration, Margaret announced that the relationship that had lasted for several years during the mid 1950s was no more. She had given in to pressure from the establishment. Although these people on New Street, Great Houghton, held a street party, just like ones for the Coronation and VE Day in earlier times, they were not to know that their good wishes would be in vain. Margaret married the photographer, Anthony Armstrong-Jones, but had only accepted his proposal the day after learning that Townsend had married someone else.

Above: Barnsley came of age in 1869 when it was incorporated as a borough. The coat of arms was designed to include the motto 'Spectemur Agendo', meaning 'Judge us by our actions'. It has seen several alterations over the years and now includes two shuttles and crossed pickaxes representing the linen and coal mining trades that were once important to the town. Figures of a miner and a glassblower stand holding the shield. In July, 1969, celebrations were held to mark the centenary of the incorporation. There was a grand procession as part of the festivities and here we can see part of it coming along Church Street. The offices of the Barnsley Chronicle are still there today. Known these days as just the Barnsley Chronicle, the newspaper was founded in 1858.

Left: A miner's daughter from Cudworth , Dorothy Hyman, won her first Commonwealth Games gold medal in 1958, aged 17, in the sprint relay. Although blessed with natural talent, she had to go to some length to exploit it. The nearest track was eight miles away. Initial training was with Eddie Fleetwood, who was second team coach at Barnsley FC, then she joined Hickleton Main Athletic Club. Between 1957 and 1963, Dorothy Hyman established herself as Britain's top woman sprinter, taking 100 metres gold and 200m silver at the European Championships of 1958, 100m silver and 200m bronze at the 1960 Olympics, followed by the 100 yds/200yds sprint double gold at the Commonwealth Games of 1962, plus a silver in the relay. In the 1964 Olympics in Tokyo she helped the Great Britain team pick up a bronze medal in the 4 x 100m relay with team mates Janet Simpson, Mary Rand and Daphne Arden. After coming second to swimmer Anita Londesborough in the 1962, BBC Sports Personality of the Year, Dorothy was deservedly crowned winner the following year. On a local level, The Dorothy Hyman Sports Centre, in Cudworth, is named in her honour.

Right: Shep's Banjo Boys struck up the music and Granada TV's popular 'The Comedians' show took to the air in the 1970s. Filmed in front of live audiences weaned on entertainers in working men's clubs, the television programme provided a new lease of life for some older comics and a wider audience for up and coming talent. There was Ken Goodwin with his 'settle down' catchphrase, Mike 'terrific' Reid and Duggie Brown and his parrot and plumber joke. Among the best of them was our very own Charlie Williams (1927-2006). Born in Royston, the son of a Barbadian who came to England in 1914 to enlist in the Royal Engineers, Charlie found initial fame as a soccer player. He was one of the first black players in professional football and played throughout his career as a centre half for Doncaster Rovers in the 1950s. Somewhat bizarrely, his only goal was scored against Barnsley. Having retired from the game, he tried his luck as a singer, but found that his chat

between songs was getting more attention than the tunes he tried to belt out. He had the good sense to concentrate on comedy and a star was born. A black comedian with a broad Yorkshire accent was a novelty and he milked it to great effect. Charlie's peak years were in the 1970s and he starred at the London Palladium, was the subject of 'This is Your Life' and hosted TV's 'The Golden Shot'. He was awarded the MBE in 1999 for his charity work. His companion on stage in this photograph, taken in his hey day, was the Mayor of Barnsley.

Below: Crowds gather in Barnsley station to photograph, or just stare at, or recall memories of a nearly forgotten sight on the railway lines of the country. The decision in 1968 by British Railways to do away with steam could have meant that the sight of a steam locomotive hauling a train was gone for ever. The efforts of steam enthusiasts paid off. The eight-day exhibition tour by the 'King George V' in 1971 was a resounding success with thousands of people flocking to see the train. As a direct consequence twelve steam-hauled trains were sanctioned to run on main lines in 1972. The return in 1973 of LNER'S the 'Flying Scotsman' from America set the seal of success on all this hard work and it became part of the band of 'limited editions' of locomotive preserved to haul excursions and undertake promotional tours round the country. One enthusiast described it thus 'There is nothing to match the awesome power of an express locomotive hauling a heavy train at main line speeds'. Look at crowds who flock to the private steam lines preserved around the country or to the railway museums for evidence of that enthusiasm.

TRANSPORT

The age of the tram helped link the rural town of Wombwell and its High Street with the outside world. Until 1959, it was also well served by two railway stations. One served what are now the Penistone and Hallam lines, while the now defunct Wombwell West linked with Doncaster. When the tramlines were laid in the early 20th century, public transport in the area provided an excellent service for both long and short haul journeys. Getting to and from somewhere like Thurnscoe involved a round trip of 10 miles, which would have been several hours spent walking. The tram did the journey there and back in well under the hour without any effort at all. Pictured in the 1920s, local residents seemed fascinated with the prospect of being snapped by the photographer. Trams operated in Barnsley from 1924 until 1933 a very short period of time

Above: The motorbus provided more flexibility than the tram, tied as the latter was to its pantograph, overhead cables and track. Eventually, the newer form of transport would see off its rival, but for some years they co-existed. This AEC bus must have been patronised by several hardy customers who were able to endure the South Yorkshire wind that could cut through you on certain days. The Associated Equipment Company, to give it a full title, is one of the best known names in the world of buses. Always shortened to its initials, it is most famously associated with its London Routemaster models. However, its influence in the field of transport is much wider than just our capital city as AEC has supplied buses and commercial vehicles both domestically and internationally. The company's ability to produce large numbers of vehicles using assembly line methods became important in supplying the increasing need for army lorries during the 1914-18 war. From then on, AEC became associated with both lorries and buses. The company changed its official name in the late 1940s to Associated Commercial Vehicles, but perversely retained the AEC logo on the vast majority of the vehicles it built. The company was bought out by Leyland in 1962. The photograph was taken in Stocksbridge, the small steel town on the old Manchester to Sheffield road.

Doncaster Road, in Goldthorpe, was a busy place in 1920. The tram service meant a much easier link with either Barnsley or Doncaster, the two nearest towns of a reasonable size. However, by the end of the decade neither town was served by trams. Yet, they had also had an impact on house building in the area as developments sprang up along the routes. Both householders and builders recognised the impact that good public transport links had on residential choice. Buses took over the routes and a little piece of transport history was consigned to the museum, but their use merely reinforced the importance of having housing that was well connected. The village of Goldthorpe has a longer history than most might expect. It is recorded in the Domesday Book as Guldetorp. Robert de Goldthorp married Elizabeth de Shepley in 1351 and their combined manors and estates established them and their descendants as one of the most prominent families in the Huddersfield and Barnsley area. Their influence was felt right through until late Tudor times. Presumably, the surname came from that of an earlier person called Gulde who lived on a farmstead, as 'thorp' or 'thorpe' is commonly used as part of a place name throughout the old Ridings.

Above: Trams were a safe form of public transport. They had cables and tracks to follow and seldom presented a threat to people's lives and limbs. However, this did not seem to be the case on 2 December, 1914. 'Blimey', one local was heard to say, 'You'd be better off in the trenches.' Whilst this was hardly true, one can understand his sentiments when looking at the aftermath of the tramcar that had raced out of control down the hill. With an injury toll of seven injured, this was one of the worst accidents of its type that the Barnsley and District Tramway ever experienced. The caped bobby looked quite nonplussed as he tried to make some sense of events. One bystander seemed to be trying to take charge as spectators with a ghoulish interest in such happenings began to gather. There must be something about the British psyche that draws us to a scene of carnage so that we can just stand and gawp. Despite the evidence of this photographs, travelling by tram was generally a safe and reliable mode of transport. The earliest vehicles were pulled by horses and the conversion to electric power did not begin until 31 October, 1902. The first route ran from Smithies, near the Monk Bretton Colliery, to Worsbrough Bridge and Worsbrough Dale. Disputes with the Great Central Railway company limited the growth of the tramway and it never realised the ambitions of its planners in its scale of operation. Barnsley was one of the first towns to abandon its network when it withdrew operations in 1930. Public transport was then given over to motor buses. The tramcar sheds on Sheffield Road were given over to garaging and servicing buses. This depot was owned later by the Stagecoach company, but was closed to make way for a housing development. It was demolished in 2009. Very little of the system survives today apart from a few sawn off overhead wire poles in the cutting on Upper Sheffield Road.

photographs were taken in or around 1948. Public transport began to get under way on a respectable scale with the introduction of trams in 1902. The expansion of services encouraged the development of housing schemes on the outskirts of the town and along the sides of the main roads. Before the turn of the century it was usual for people to live within easy walking distance of their place of employment - and this led to some crowded and cramped low-quality dwellings being constructed near to industrial areas. The growth in the provision and use of public transport in Barnsley, along with increases in the number of cars in the area, resulted in terrific congestion on town centre streets. This was not unique to Barnsley; similar conditions were being experienced in every developing town in the country as the population became more mobile and more affluent. Shopping areas were becoming more centralised and action was needed to speed the flow of shoppers and workers in and out of every town. One major step in the right direction was the decision to construct a new bus station which would ease the situation by taking bus stands (and the associated queues of waiting passengers) off the streets of the town centre and into a well-equipped and purpose-built site. Work began in 1937 with the excavation of over 11,000 tons of material to form a spacious, level site. When the new facility opened in 1938 it was acclaimed as one of the best bus stations in the county, boasting progressive features such as toilets with hot and cold running water, and a catering section considered to be 'the best in the business'.

Bottom left: The Yorkshire Traction double decker in the photograph is seen on the morning of 21 January, 1950, heading into Regent Street towards the Congregational Church, built in 1856. It is about to pass the old Post Office. Solicitors and firms offering financial services occupy many of the buildings along this part of Regent Street. Parts of it now look rather drab and gloomy. The single decker turning into Church Street bore the registration letters HE. These showed that it had first been registered in Barnsley. The motor cyclist on the right was well wrapped up against the weather, but his headgear was quite lightweight. Compulsory crash helmets were some way in the future.

Above and below: Truly atmospheric scenes dating from just a few short years after the end of the Second World War. The pictures show the bus station in full-swing, with a mixture of single deck and double deck vehicles guaranteed to evoke feelings of nostalgia in both young and old. It is thought that the

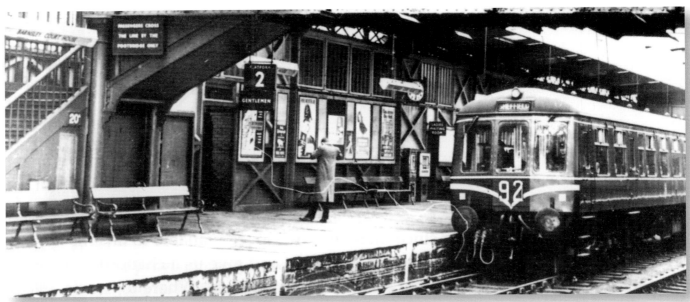

Above: A sad day for rail enthusiasts and the travelling public is reflected in this photograph taken on 17 April, 1960. The reason being that this was the last day of passenger services from Court House Station, in Barnsley, an all-too familiar occurrence at hundreds of smaller railway stations up and down the land in the 1960s. In this scene a multiple-unit diesel can be seen waiting at the station platform. At the time the station was almost a century old. As the name suggested, it had been built originally as a courthouse, having been opened in 1861. Its function as a railway station began in 1870.

Just five years before the closure it had been the subject of an extensive modernisation programme which involved the replacement of canopies and lighting.

Below: Ten years earlier around 1950 this 0-6-0 Johnson tank Locomotive 58075 with a push and pull set, waits patiently in Barnsley Courthouse Station, building up a head of steam before moving off. This particular model was built in early 1895. Sadly, retirement was not far round the corner and final disposal came in 1953.

Right: The lower end of Regent Street in February, 1950, with the iron span of the railway bridge carrying an advertisement for one of the town's more famous shops. That bridge has gone now, demolished in 1961, but there is still evidence of its existence with the wall and pillar to be seen. The reason why the Court House Station closed was that the railway bridge which crossed Elton Road was going to cost so much to repair; it was cheaper to close the station and move to Exchange Station nearby. Across the road from the Court House is the imposing front of the Queen's Hotel. Opened in 1885, it was, like many other hotels built at the time, designed to serve the rail travelling public as passenger numbers increased due to the rapid expansion of the system.

Below: A Class Five steam locomotive 4-6-0 number 44971 leaving Cudworth in September, 1967, on the run from Sheffield to Leeds. There were 842 Class Five locomotives built for the old LMS and were popularly known as 'Black Fives'. The magic of steam to many people is indefinable and to them the steam locomotive is almost a living thing. It is not just about collecting engine numbers, a hobby many a young lad would do before he developed other interests, but

something one steam fan calls 'an incurable disease'. When the curtain was finally rung down on steam on British Railways in August, 1968, shortly after this photograph was taken, it was decreed that no preserved steam locomotive would be allowed to run on British Rail

lines. The powers of British Rail, however, did not reckon with the enthusiasm and determination of steam preservation societies and three years later one steam locomotive undertook an-eight-day exhibition tour and thousands of people flocked to see it. Thus began a movement which has not stopped growing since.

BIRD'S EYE VIEW

Below: The general view of Town End was taken from the top of Pinfold Hill. The photographer stood at a spot where there was once a compound where, in medieval times, stray animals were collected and kept. The owner than had to pay a fine for their release. In later times, the pinfold was used by a drover to hold his animals temporarily whilst on the way to market. The scene here shows the industrial nature of Barnsley just before the First World War when the smoking mill chimneys provide the sort of inspiration that the Salford artist LS Lowry would have loved to have drawn upon. You can almost visualise matchstalk men and matchstalk cats and dogs down below. The flags flying on the building on the left belonged to the Olympia Skating Rink. The small park in the foreground opened on 29 June 1905, amid much ceremony. Having somewhere to relax and play in such a built up environment was a great boon. It helped locals break out from the monotony and drabness of their everyday surroundings. Looking at this photograph really does help us to think that William Blake got it right when he wrote 'Jerusalem'. Even though the poem was written a century before it was taken, the term 'dark, satanic mills' still rang true.

Above: Penistone is now a comfortable village or small town of about 10,000 inhabitants. It has always had some significance in the area and was well known enough over 900 years ago to gain mention in the Domesday Book. In the 19th century it became an important railway junction. In the 1950s, its Woodhead Line was the first in the country to be electrified, but this was controversially closed in 1981, the track lifted and, latterly, became used as a cycling and walking trail. The old Cloth Hall is one of the main Penistone buildings of historical interest. Locals made woollen goods as far back as the 15th century. The Cloth Hall designed and built by John Platt at a cost of £800, opened in 1763. However, a decline in trade meant that it served little purpose by the middle of the next century and was turned into shops and the White Bear beerhouse. It also housed an early Post Office and was the base for the British Legion for about 40 years from 1926 onwards. A chemist used the premises more recently. Penistone Church is another significant building. Some of the masonry in St John the Baptist is over 1,000 years old and traces of a Saxon cross have been found here. The handsome square tower dates from around 1500, though the stainless steel fish shaped weather vane was only added in 1975. It is a Grade I listed building.

Above: Lovely buildings like this complextha was Barnsley had their own special character. The concrete, steel and glass monstrosities, all sharp corners and right angles, that dominated the style of new schools in the 1960s and 1970s, have little or no personalities. Parents and pupils were happy with the old order, with the vast majority wanting single sex schools where expectations were high and standards naturally reflected them. It is debatable as to whether or not they were the best years as some would have you believe, but they were certainly among the most memorable. Girls who are now well established pensioners can still recall the 1950s with Miss Baldwin as headmistress and the work set by Miss Darbyshire as form mistress. It was not all study and homework as there were great times on the hockey field and netball court, not to mention physical jerks during PT in the gym. It had flourished for much of the last century since opening in Queens Road in 1905 in the former Conservative Club when Miss AJ Robinson was the head, before moving to this site in 1909. Nicknamed 'Buckingham Palace', it was turned into a Sixth Form College in the mid 1970s before closing in 2001.

Left: The houses were so close to one another that you could hear your neighbour tapping on his eggshell at breakfast time. Living almost in one another's pockets meant that there were few secrets. They all knew each other's business. But, there was a good side to such communities. Provided you were honest in your dealings, a neighbour never let you down. There was always a friendly hand to help out if things got tough. They kept an eye out for each other. Had there been a motorway in 1933, then we would be looking towards the M1 in this photograph, gazing across the junction of Park Grove and Hawthorne Street in the foreground, with Park Road in the centre and old Agnes Road School, that closed in 1992, to the left.

Below: An aerial view of Barnsley showing a sea of terraced houses which were the homes of thousands of local residents. The photograph was taken in 1933. The camera was directed to the south-east in order to capture this scene. The junction of Park Grove and Hawthorne Street can be seen in the foreground and Agnes Road School is featured in the left hand corner of the picture. Park Road is the main road running left to right in the centre of the scene. This was the heart of suburban, working class Barnsley in the 1930s, an area containing virtually everything that residents needed for their daily lives, scores of small family-run shops offering all the products and services necessary at the time. Public houses and other places of entertainment completed the picture of daily life in the time of our parents and grandparents.

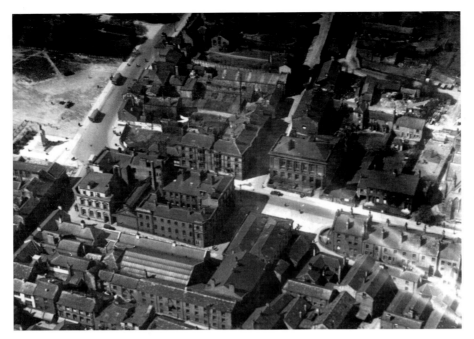

Left: The aerial view was taken in May, 1928. It shows Regent Street, Church Street and Eastgate. An area has already been cleared so that work on the building of the Town Hall and College of Technology can begin. Experience gained in the First World War had promoted the use of aeroplanes to assist in the mapping and development of our towns. Aviation pioneers, flying their flimsy machines over enemy lines in order to obtain up-to-the-minute military reconnaissance to help the war effort, got an invaluable grounding in the art of photography from on high. There was a large amount of commercial work available in peacetime as the aviation industry entered an age when it developed by leaps and bounds. An aerial perspective gave town planners an extra way of looking at a problem or checking for solutions.

Left and above: The lower parts of this 1968 view of Barnsley on the left, shortly before re-development altered the face of much of the town centre, is taken up with the town's industry. The Electricity and Gas Works round Gas Nook stand on one side of the rail line and over the level crossing on the other are the CEAG premises. May Day Green and the market with the Cross Keys Inn lead us past the Burlington Arcade towards the market stalls on Market Hill and then to Shambles Street. On the other side of the Town Hall is the Technical College. Victoria Road and Huddersfield Road lead to new Technical College buildings. Opposite the Civic Hall is Eldon Arcade and at the end of Eldon Street at the corner of Regent Street is the Queen's Hotel but the Court House Railway Station had been taken out of use the previous year. To complete the picture is the white-topped, purpose-built bowling alley, with the Baba club at the bottom end. In the picture above from 1977 the skyline has started to change. The area between Shambles Street and Westgate is the site of John Rideal House, Westgate Plaza, the five storey building which is home to Barnsley Council.

The Railway Bridge across Eldon Street from the Court House Station gives a lead to our tour of central Barnsley in the 1950s. The market's popularity is at its height here and we can see the extent to which it dominated this part of the town. On the other side of May Day Green is the old Littlewoods store and close by are the Corporation Buildings. Woolworth's original store on Queen Street backs up to Eldon Street and at the top corner where both streets meet is the unique frontage of Burtons. The extent to which the Public Hall dominates the central area is plain to see here as is the majesty of the Regent Street Congregational Church. The Court House to the left of the church still retains its function but the buildings today on the street do not possess the same authority as those when this photograph was taken. Barnsley Building Society and the businesses of Market Hill take us back to Queen Street and the old Yorkshire Bank premises. On the opposite corner is Market Street, looking more imposing here from this height than it does at ground level today. No Town Hall to dominate this photograph, just the area of the town for which Barnsley was renowned - the Market.

WORKING LIFE

Below: Although it was not the first co-operative society, the Rochdale Pioneers Equitable Society was the first to establish fully the ideas and practices that were soon copied by other similar groups across the country. The original shop, now a museum, opened on Rochdale's Toad Lane in 1844. It became the prototype for all others. The mechanisation of traditional work during the industrial revolution brought poverty to the door of many whose craft was steeped in the past. About 28 weavers and other Southeast Lancashire artisans banded together to sell items of food that they could not otherwise afford. By buying in bulk, they were able to gain discounts and pass these savings on to other members of their co-operative. Other profits were paid as a dividend and, over the years, this became known colloquially as the

'divvi'. As with many new ventures, the initial times were a struggle, but the founders persevered. The first goods on sale were limited to butter, sugar, oatmeal and candles. Gradually, business increased and tea and tobacco were added to the list. The Pioneers gained a reputation for honesty and fairness in their dealings and the food and provisions they supplied were of a good quality. Pictured in 1875, this was the first Co-operative shop in Barnsley. It opened in 1862 at 16 Market Street.

Above: Radio was to be the new medium that would revolutionise home entertainment. In the early 1920s, the Co-operative Society opened its own wireless shop. All the modern paraphernalia of valves, speakers, vacuum tubes, receivers and transmitters were there on show. To the uninitiated, it was a marvel of modern engineering, an Aladdin's cave of wonder. The transformation in our homes was similar to the changes that personal computers would bring in the late 1990s and early 2000s. Communication by telegraph was achieved by Samuel Morse in the 1840s, but experiment with wireless telegraphy did not fully bear fruit until the 1890s. Work by such pioneers as Edison and Marconi led to the latter being able to operate an early radio station on the Isle of Wight in 1897 and found a 'wireless' factory in Chelmsford a year later. The first BBC transmission came from station 2LO, based in Marconi House, London. 'Children's Hour' was one of the earliest of programmes and as word spread about the new medium,

Left: Barnsley Co-operative Society celebrated its diamond jubilee in 1922. This display was mounted to reflect the importance of the occasion. Members of staff dressed for the part and the whole interior looked a treat with beautifully dressed mannequins, draped curtains, potted plants and chandeliers sparkling in the electric light. The whole organisation had come a long way from the little shopkeeper's establishment on the other side of the Pennines when the first slab of butter was sold and the first few ounces of sugar weighed.

Below: The Barnsley British Co-operative Society, incorporating its Drapery Stores, was celebrating its 90th anniversary in 1952. By then, the little shop further down Market Street had been left behind in favour of the

people began to save up for these newfangled receivers. Gradually, prices became more affordable and, in the 1930s, most homes had a set around which families would sit in an evening. Jack Payne and Henry Hall led the immensely popular BBC Dance Orchestra to cater for the demand for light entertainment.

magnificent Arcadia House at 72-74 Market Street, on Island Corner at the junction with New Street and Wellington Street. Tremendous buildings such as this one laugh at the puny attempts of constructions dominated by steel, glass and prefabricated concrete to act as any form of artistic or aesthetic rivals.

Above: The butchery at the Barnsley British Co-operative Society stood on Market Street. In 1904, a group of employees stood proudly below the birds that had been hung there to season and develop a proper gamey taste. The sight of so much raw meat out in the open air will give supporters of the health and safety club an apoplectic fit. Yet, this was how a proper butcher's shop looked. Our grandfathers did not collapse, laid low by mysterious bugs that are supposed to infest such produce. Once upon a time, you could see hares and rabbits hanging on hooks, just as they are here, but they also seem to be things of the past as well. This building was erected on the corner with Wellington Street. Some of the ceramic work is very attractive,

with human heads set in ribbed pilasters and a large, sculpted lion at the apex above the main entrance. There are also gryphons to admire on the sort of grand edifice that we no longer erect in our towns.

Bottom left: The Prince of Wales, the future Edward VIII, was coming to town. Brothers Albert and John Hirst decided to prepare a meal fit for a future king on the day that he was due to officiate at the official opening of the Town Hall in 1933. A Barnsley chop was one of the selected cuts of meat and the proud butchers made sure that their royal guest feasted off the best. This particular delicacy is thought to have originated in the King's Head Hotel, later the NatWest Bank, when hungry farmers lunched well after coming to town on market day, requiring some major sustenance before embarking on the journey back home. An alternative claim to its origin is also made by the Brooklands Hotel. The cut is taken right across the loin, creating a double-sided chop. Albert Hirst was especially well known for his black puddings that were christened 'the north's caviar'. Letters simply

addressed to 'the black pudding king' found their way to him. The meal that he and his brother prepared for Prince Edward in the kitchen of the Royal Hotel was presented to him with all the trimmings. However, it is reported that the heir to the throne nearly fainted when he realised that the 3lb of lamb in front of him was meant for his delectation alone.

Below: It may be hard to imagine today, but in the 1890s, if you were injured, it was left to the police, firefighters and even taxi-drivers to staff a fleet of wheeled stretchers, named 'litters', to take patients to the nearest hospital or doctor's surgery. A full-time ambulance service was only established shortly before the turn of the 20th century. This image taken in 1912 looks like the scene from an amateur magic trick that has gone horribly wrong. It is however a very basic first-aid training session at the ambulance station in Goldthorpe. This training was to prove to be very significant a few years later at the onset of the First World War. This year was significant as the last for the use of horse drawn ambulances.

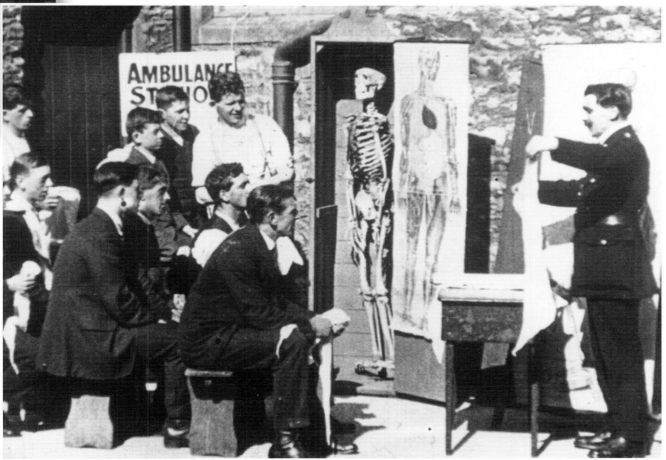

Above: Looking somewhat sombre in his pose, holding the reins of his faithful partner in work, JC Tinker was the last cabman of his type to be seen in the town. Motorised cabs saw to it that the days of his horse drawn business were numbered. His style of transport for hire was consigned to the museum and a way of life went into the history books. It is only surprising that it took until 1919 for time to catch up with Mr Tinker. The Marlborough Hotel, 36 Dodworth Road, provided the backdrop for the photograph and it was form here that he had taken home many a soul who had supped long but none too wisely. The hostelry, situated not far from the large roundabout on the western part of the ring road, is still trading today. The Marlborough was formerly known as the Boy and Barrel.

Left: Housekeeping and raising a family were considered ideal female roles during the 1950s, although that standard was less rigid than in previous decades. With marriage and birth rates booming, women were becoming wives and mothers at unprecedented levels. But more women were entering the work-place as well. During World War II women took factory jobs to make up for the domestic manpower shortage. After the war the number of working women dropped, but by 1950 it was climbing again, at the rate of a million a year. These three factory workers from Woods Brothers Glass Works formed part of these statistics, when this photograph was taken at the Pontefract

Road site in 1952. About 1900 a branch of the works had been set up in Wombwell but the main site was at Pontefract Road, in Barnsley, where the works expanded to build up a reputation for a wide variety of products, pressed and blown, domestic and industrial. The business was closed in February, 1981.

Below: 'The Dustbinmen', a television sitcom written by Jack Rosenthal, was briefly popular in 1969-70. Starring Bryan Pringle, Graham Haberfield and Trevor Bannister, it told of the lives, skives and loves of a group of men in the local council's employment. Various epithets have been given to the job that real workers carry out. A waste disposal operative is one of the more laughable descriptions that become even more derisory when the men themselves describe their role as being 'on the bins'. In early pre-industrial times waste was mainly composed of ash from fires, wood, bones, carcases and vegetable waste. It was disposed of in the ground where it would act as compost and help to improve the soil. Some landfill sites were created, but it

was largely left to individual choice whether or not to use them. In medieval times, most waste was burned on household fires. The first attempts at legislation on the removal of rubbish from homes were made in the 15th century. A court record of 1515 from Stratford-upon-Avon shows that Shakespeare's father was fined for depositing waste in the street! It was during the industrial revolution that an increased volume of unwanted material became a problem, though it did provide opportunities for the quaintest of jobs. 'Toshers' worked in sewers, scavenging for coins and metal. 'Mudlarks' looked for disposed of items on river banks and 'dustmen' collected ash from fires for use in brick making or as a soil conditioner. The 1848 Public Health Act began the regulation of waste disposal. Another Act in 1875 charged local authorities with a statutory duty of removing it from homes and making it safe in dumps, mass incinerators or landfill sites. Here, George Grant and Walter Robinson are standing alongside the first of the town's motorised dustcarts that was introduced into service in the 1920s.

Above and below: Fire appliances have developed greatly over the years and the two engines shown on this page are particularly fine examples. The 80 foot fire escape ladder was one of the main features of the Leyland fire engine that was the pride and joy of Barnsley Fire Brigade. The photograph above can be dated fairly accurately as the Town Hall can be seen in the background during its period of construction in 1932-33. Churchfield Inspector Weatherhogg and five of his volunteer officers posed proudly, as befitted their importance in seeing to it that the general public and its property was in safe hands whenever the worst happened and homes and businesses were ablaze. Until mid-Victorian times, firefighting was a haphazard process. It was not until the Metropolitan Fire Brigade Act was passed in 1865 that legislation for the provision of this resource was taken away from insurance companies and given to local authorities. Even so, it was not until 1938 that the latter was legally bound to provide such a service.

Below: Wartime women NFS officer's wore navy woollen suits with either trousers or a skirt. They were also issued with steel helmets for protection and a soft fabric peak cap that was worn around the station. Women undertook some training, but did not fight fires in the Second World War. They became fire watchers and drivers, managed the communications network and worked in mobile canteen vans. Many women received awards for their remarkable achievements during this time. At the end of the war, the majority of women were discharged from the fire service. Extremely important to the Barnsley Borough Fire Brigade were the six ladies enjoying a tea break in this 1960s photograph. Although not fighting fires, their communications role in the control room at the new Broadway Fire Station was key to saving lives, ensuring a swift and accurate response from the fire tenders and crews. The firewomen besplendant in their uniforms are from left to right; Mary Long, Mary Betts, Joyce Fuller, Kath Reynolds, Julie Beard and Ethel Brisbane.

Above: A sight that could have been a tragedy for many a citizen of Barnsley in 1960 was that of Eddy Burton's well known fish and chip shop at the corner of Eldon Street and Beckett Street appearing to go up in flames. The fire was caused by the dripping overheating and catching fire. The amount of smoke that this naturally caused, especially as the shop used a gas fired range, made it seem worse than it was and it was not long before members of the Barnsley Borough Fire Brigade, with their appliances ready to save a landmark in the town, had it all under control with nothing more than smoke damage to the shop and the upstairs rooms. To the relief of the many devotees of Burton's fish and chips, the shop was able to re-open for business the following day after massive efforts to clean up the mess.

Some people refer to oil as being 'black gold', but to Yorkshire folk it means coal. At one time, Barnsley and its satellite districts relied on the mining industry for their very being. There is evidence that mining took place in the Silkstone area 200 years before the Battle of Hastings and the Norman Conquest. It is a recorded fact that the monks at Pontefract Priory paid the grand sum of £8 for a Barnsley pit in 1491 and ran it for about 16 years. Much of the land that held the coal was owned by the Crown until the late 17th century, though mining rights were usually granted to the local population. As well as the obvious fuel for domestic hearths, coal was in heavy demand by trades such as breweries, furnaces and smithies. There was so much coal under our feet that Barnsley was able to supply a wide area beyond its boundaries, but it needed a decent transport system to back up this industry. Consequently, two canals and four railway lines were built to provide the necessary support. By the start of the 20th century, coal was the town's premier industry.

This was the peak period for coal. By the start of World War I, national production stood at a mighty 280 million tons, of which a third was exported. The industry employed about a million men and boys, but it was terribly dangerous

work. The Barnsley seam was particularly susceptible to the production of firedamp or methane gas, a notably volatile substance that was lethal when a sizeable volume of it built up as it only took a spark from a pick to ignite it with terrifying consequences. As colliery owners searched out bigger and better seams of coal, they had to go deeper and further afield. As they reached out to more rural areas it was necessary to provide homes for the workforce. Dedicated pit villages were built and almost the whole population relied on the mine for its livelihood. This meant that families formed a very tight and supportive community. This was especially noticeable whenever disaster struck or men were laid off. Examples of this togetherness were seen in recent times during the miners' strikes and periods of industrial unrest in the 1980s. Part of the action in the movie 'Billy Elliot' looks at this period in our history and some of the scenes were shot in Easington, County Durham. Another film, 'Brassed Off', was even more focused on life in a pit village at a similar time. The action was shot in and around Grimethorpe. Coal mining has always been one of the most difficult of jobs. The miner's life expectancy was 10 years less than that of a white collar worker. The sheer volume of muck and filth that he encountered meant that his pores and nails became ingrained with coal that could not be removed, however hard he scrubbed himself in the tin bath in front of the fire. Living conditions varied considerably. The quality of the housing was often dependent on the size and prosperity of the owners. Some employers, especially those with large landed estates, took a strongly paternalistic attitude towards their colliers. At the beginning of the 20th century training became more important because of advances in the tools and machinery. Every man who entered the coal industry underwent a course of instruction for a minimum specified period until he could do the job. According to the 1981 census, the village of Grimethorpe had 44 per cent of its workers employed in the mining industry. This pit was one of the deepest in the country, but its closure in 1993 took the heart out of the village. The band plays on, but with a mournful note. Houghton Main was another important colliery, just northeast of Darfield. It opened in 1875. The River Dearne flows between the pit and the village and was notorious for flooding. Sometimes men had to remove their socks and clogs as they waded through the water before river improvements were

COAL! COAL! COAL

The NATION requires 24,000,000 ton more Coal this year.
Are YOU doing YOUR SHARE?

COAL for MUNITIONS MAKING
COAL for MINESWEEPERS
COAL for ELECTRICITY WORKS
COAL for GAS WORKS
COAL for COKE WORKS
COAL for STEEL MAKING
COAL for SHIPS, bringing FOOD, GUNS and PLANES for you

HOUGHTON MAIN is supplying Coal for all these urposes, and Maximum Output is demanded of us

Are YOU doing your best to defeat the enemy?

carried out in the late 1960s. The huge slag heaps were a horrid blight on the landscape, but they were reclaimed in the early 1980s. At its peak in the early 20th century, Houghton Main employed well over 2,000 people. It was one of the last of the area's mines to close. Elsecar Main Colliery (below) was situated in the vicinity of workings that dated back to the 1600s. However, it was not until 1905 that mining as we know it began here. Shafts were sunk to the Parkgate seam, with others sunk to work the Silkstone, Thorncliffe and Swallow Wood seams. At one time, the colliery was producing 400,000 tons per annum. Miners worked hard extracting the coal, so it was no surprise that some of them enjoyed a cooling dip in the canal on lighter moments. Barnsley's position as a prominent player in the coal industry remained constant until the mid 1940s when the seams began to be exhausted. Mining continued in 24 remaining seams, but by the 1970s the first sounds of the death knell were heard. The nails in the coffin were firmly rammed home during the strikes and painful disputes of the mid 1980s as closure came after closure.

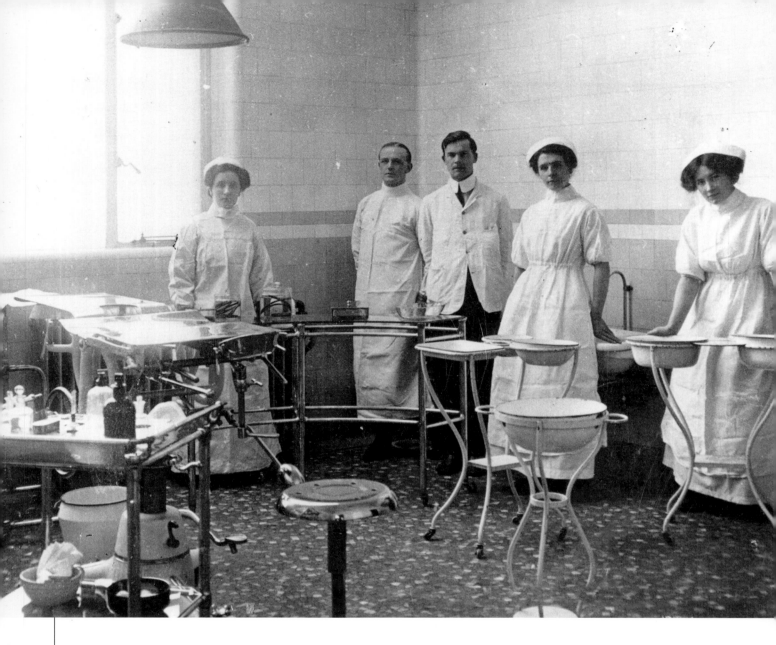

This was the new operating theatre at Barnsley's Beckett Hospital. The doctors and nurses were very proud of their up-to-the minute-equipment that offered the best possible care for all the patients who might come under the surgeon's knife. It might not have been 'Casualty' or 'Holby City', but this was as good as it got at in 1937. Compared with modern medicine, the techniques were old fashioned, the equipment primitive and drugs limited. Everyday penicillin was not discovered until 1928 and was not put into general use until the 1940s. What now appear as minor diseases, for example scarlet fever, whooping cough and measles, were once killers. This hospital was founded in Church Lane on 14 March, 1865, by John

Staniforth Beckett. His aim was to provide treatment, medicines and medical advice for those who found themselves in poverty. An extension was built in 1900 to create an 18-bed ward that offered specialist care for children. The nurses in the picture may not have carried lamps as Florence Nightingale did, but they were angels of mercy nonetheless. The team of professionals included Theatre Sister Ryan and nurses England and Lindley. One of their busiest times was when they assisted Doctors Fitzgerald and Watson as they helped the surgeon Doctor Isaac Rose deal with miners injured in the Wharncliffe Woodmoor pit disaster of 1936, when 58 lost their lives. The hospital closed in 1977 and was demolished two years later.

Barnsley Lock & Safe Co. Ltd - A Name to Trust

Barnsley Lock & Safe Co. Ltd is Yorkshire's premier locksmith and security company. The firm has been in business since 1972. Roy Stuart Broadhead (Stuart) started his own joinery business in 1969 after working as a farm hand, lorry driver and miner. He relocated the business from his garage to premises in Kexborough in 1972 and, with his wife Megan, expanded into DIY and hardware. Stuart soon found there was a demand for security products and locksmith services from local colleries.

Following a decline in demand for joinery, the business relocated to Darton in 1976. Still trading under his own name, 'R.S.Broadhead', more staff were employed enabling Stuart to specialise in locksmithing.

After joining the Master Locksmiths Association, the demand for locksmith services and security equipment increased. Stuart opened a new branch, 'Barnsley Lock & Safe Company' in 1979 at 44 Doncaster Road, in Barnsley.

The Darton branch was sold in 1983. In the early 1980s both of Stuart and Megan's sons, Colin and Graham, joined the business.

The business moved to the current premises, 17 Doncaster Road, Barnsley (The Alhambra Service Garage), in 1990, offering a large car park, showroom, offices and workshop facilities. This move enabled the company to employ more staff and start manufacturing its own locking devices. The acclaimed 'Limpet' vehicle lock was launched in 1993, the first locking device to be produced by the company. Stuart's decision to start manufacturing was fortuitous when the following year the last of the Yorkshire coal mines closed.

Stuart and Megan retired in 1998 leaving the business in the capable hands of their sons. Today, Barnsley Lock & Safe Co. Ltd. is still a family run business, now employing eight staff, offering all locksmith services, expert key cutting, all makes of locks, access control and safes. Through skill, knowledge, flexibility and excellent value the company has obtained nationwide contracts with local authorities, high street banks and retailers. With staff offering well over 100 years of combined experience, Barnsley Lock & Safe Co. Ltd provides the people of Barnsley with the highest level of service, and, above all, security from a name to trust.

Top: The R.S. Broadhead premises in Kexborough in 1972.
*Above: Trade counter staff pictured in 2001. **Below:** Barnsley Lock & Safe Co. Ltd's 17 Doncaster Road, Barnsley, premises in 2010.*

A Dimension in Time. . . .

Dimensions Training Solutions Ltd, based at Archway House, Barnsley, has been responsible for the training of thousands of hairdressers over the past three decades.

On 21 May, 1973, Dimensions Hairdressing was opened in Peel Street Arcade, Barnsley, by Bill Shaw and Jon Major who were at the time just 19 and 20 years old. The partners had met at hairdressing college and had remained close friends before joining forces to open their own premises on the site of a former dress shop and ladies' hairdressing salon known as Ritas.

Mr Hasty, the agent from Wilbys, who the boys approached looking for an empty unit to turn into a modern, trendy

hairdressing salon - the first unisex salon in Barnsley - did a brilliant selling job.

From the very beginning Dimensions was going to be different: it was a time of radical change with the trend switching from the traditional shampoo-and-set clientele to the newer 'precision cutting' and blow drying. This was right where Bill and Jon wanted to be.

The two lads caused a stir, particularly on the mens side of the business: it was 1973 and they were asking men to make an appointment for a haircut. And that wasn't all, if you wanted a haircut at Dimensions, not only did you have to make an appointment, you had to have your hair shampooed!

This was neither a gimmick nor a sales tactic, it was simply the fact that the type of hairstyling Dimensions was to become known for required hair to be cut wet and then blow dried into shape. This didn't suit everyone, but it was the right decision, with the salon soon becoming fully booked with clients who had previously been going to Leeds and Sheffield to get the kind of

Top: *Founders, Bill Shaw and Jon Major in the early 1970s.* **Left and below:** *Bill and Jon taking a break outside their first shop in Peel Street Arcade, Barnsley, also pictured below.*

both areas. This attracted two quite different responses: lots of interest and places booked on evening courses that would eventually run four nights a week in both areas; in constrast some small-minded salon owners simply tore the literature up into little pieces before wasting a stamp and posting them back.

hairdressing now being offered in Barnsley.

These were fun times for Bill and Jon who worked hard, and played just as hard in the pubs and clubs of Barnsley.

Business was however, undoubtedly easier in the early 1970s as things like business plans and cash flows were words that hadn't been invented. Word spread about what Dimensions was doing and the salon gained a steady stream of clients travelling from Leeds and Wakefield.

In 1976 a Dimensions Salon in Leeds was opened right in the centre of the city opposite the Corn Exchange. This was followed by a salon in Pontefract in 1979 and in Wakefield in 1982. More salons followed in Sheffield, Castleford, Horsforth and Meanwood (Leeds). The fun days were over and business plans and cash flows were very much part of the day-to-day life.

With the opening of the Leeds Salon the partners decided to start sharing their skills learned on the many trips to academies such as Vidal Sassoon, Tony & Guy and Alan International in London. In September, 1976, Dimensions started to offer 'Advanced Cutting Classes' in both Barnsley and Leeds, sending mail shots to all the salons in

In 1977 Bill met his beautiful wife Bernadette, also a hairdresser, who shared his vision and enthusiasm for both business and hairdressing. The original gang of two became a gang of three. The trio worked happily and tirelessly to expand the business.

Business took an interesting twist in 1978 when, following an exhibition at the Royal Lancaster Hotel in London where Dimensions had a stand to promote its Advanced Cutting Courses, a large national distributor asked if Dimensions would be interested in demonstrating a new colouring product it was launching: a new natural product called 'Henna'.

The hairdressing business from Barnsley was being asked to launch a product that would eventually go on to become a worldwide phenomenon. The highspot of this product promotion was a trip to Iceland demonstrating Henna to hairdressers in Reykjavik. A fee was

*Top, three pictures: Where the magic happened, early views inside the Dimensions salon. **Left:** Bernadette, Bill's wife, pictured in the early 1980s. Notice the star in Bernadette's hair. A stencil from a successful coloured hairspray product of the company's around this time.*

negotiated of £400 plus expenses for Bill, Jon and Bernadette. It seemed like a small fortune.

Little did the trio know how large companies worked – not least how they made sure they got value for money. Where previously the three had worked on demonstrations together, with Bernadette doing all the hard work backstage, and the boys basking in all the glory on stage, now the team was split up for separate demonstrations in different locations on each of the four days in Iceland. The boys were on their own! It was hard work but fun. Bill has a vague recollection that all three of them spent virtually the whole fee on some spectacular Icelandic woollen sweaters!

Working on the launch of Henna had wet appetites. In 1981 their own product company was formed: Bill, Jon and Bernadette

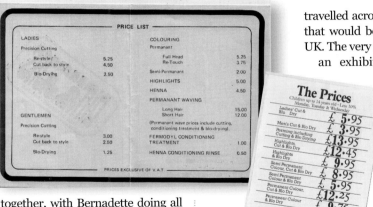

travelled across Europe looking for products that would be of interest back home in the UK. The very first they found was the best. At an exhibition in Holland a coloured hairspray was being demonstrated using stencils to put stars, moon, lightening flashes and the likes onto both hair and skin - less than a month later Bill, Jon and Bernadette sold out their entire stock on the first day of a three day exhibition at Earls Court. They had to travel through the night to Belgium for more stock for the following two days. That sold out as well.

That first diversion into products saw the trio travelling not only across Europe but also to America looking for products and at the same time see exactly what was happening across the world in hairdressing.

In 1983, with the demand for the Advanced Cutting Courses slowing down, as almost every local salon had learned the skills needed to offer clients cut and blow dries, yet another twist of fate occurred. The recession was biting and unemployment was at an all-time high. The Government announced a new programme of training for school leavers, The Youth Training Scheme. Dimensions opened its first hairdressing school (the night classes had been delivered in the salons) in Kirkgate, Wakefield, with 60 students on the brand new Youth Training Scheme (YTS) funded by the Manpower Services Commission.

Top: 1970s and 1980s Dimensions price lists. **Left:** *Dimensions Tuition Centre Programme 1978/79.* **Above:** *1980s advertising.*

Also around this time Bill became a Director of the Hairdressing Training Board which went on to become the Hairdressing And Beauty Industry Authority (HABIA) where he is now the longest serving Director and still has an active involvement as Treasurer and on various committees.

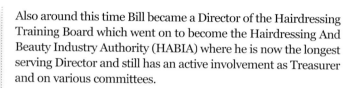

In 1995, Bill was asked to deliver Management Training Courses at the magnificent Goldwell Academy in London's Mayfair. The lad from Barnsley was now sharing his hard hitting management theories and systems with hairdressers from all over the UK. Bill had professional recordings made of his lectures and philosophy: although never a number one hit, over 1,000 copies were sold to hairdressers across the UK. Despite the passage of time those management principles still apply today.

By 1996 however, Bill was getting itchy feet again and he decided to open a 10,000 square foot hairdressing 'Cash & Carry', along with a hairdressing furniture showroom in a

That first contract was for £37,000, a small fortune compared to the amount the business had been charging for its part-time courses, where the most ever earned in a single year was around £10,000. The Wakefield school was quickly followed by similar contracts in Barnsley, Leeds and York.

Between 1983 and 1988 more salons opened in Sheffield, Horsforth and York. The training side of the business was also growing; the two founders almost by default now started to take on separate roles and responsibilities. Bill had stopped cutting hair in the salon quite some time before Jon decided to 'hang up his scissors'. Jon took on all responsibility for the day-to-day running of the salons whilst Bill focussed on training.

In 1988 however, Jon decided to 'sail off into the sunset' initially to Spain for seven years before moving to Australia where he met his wife Lally. Today the couple live in Freemantle, Western Australia.

Bill had some serious decisions to make about the future of the business. The next five years were spent selling, franchising and not renewing leases on the majority of the salons that had been built up over 15 years. This allowed the company to consolidate its position in Government-funded training.

Top left: *Hairstyles from the 1980s.* **Above**: *Dimensions promotional leaflet for their Youth Training Programme.* **Below left**: *Jon Major, who to this day, is still enjoying the good life down under.* **Below**: *The cover of Bill Shaw's Motivation & Goal Setting cassette.*

business park alongside the Meadowhall Shopping Centre in Sheffield.

£250,000 later the luxurious cash & carry was completed with coffee shop, where hairdressers could call in for their stock and have a sit down and a coffee. Bill knew right from the beginning that he wouldn't be able to compete on price with the large cash & carry groups which had much more buying power, but believed that most hairdressers would pay a 'copper or two' more and enjoy the ambiance of a nice place to visit. Bill got it completely wrong. He discovered that what was important to most salon owners was price, price and price! The cash & carry lasted three years before being closed.

Bill now turned his energies back to training with a renewed enthusiasm and passion for the business, along with a new commercial acumen developed over the previous three years. This new found commercialism enabled the training side of the business to grow beyond recognition.

From the beginning Bill took an active part in the industry's trade association and this became much more

serious when he became Worthy Master of the Guild of Hairdressers for the whole of the UK. This saw Bill representing the hairdressing industry at various events for 3 years which included a proud moment when through the association with the Guild of Hairdressers Bill and Bernadette were invited to the Queens Garden Party at Buckingham Palace.

In 2005, Bill realised an opportunity that he had longed for ever since the training business had started. When he was 15 years old and knew he wanted to be a hairdresser and had attended evening courses at his local hairdressing college: he had always wanted Dimensions Training Solutions to be the same. In 2005 Dimensions began to offer courses to young people in year 11 at school. By 2006 many schools had become seriously involved in vocational training and hairdressing was one of the more popular choices. Bill realised that the company's academies in Barnsley, Leeds, Wakefield and Sheffield were not going to be able to cope with the number of students coming from schools and had another of his great ideas, "Let's open Hairdressing Academies in schools - if the school can give us a decent size classroom, we'll invest the money from profits and turn the classroom into a fantastic commercial looking hairdressing salon."

EⅡR

The Lord Chamberlain is commanded by Her Majesty to invite

Mr. and Mrs. William Shaw

to a Garden Party at Buckingham Palace on Thursday, 11th July, 1991, from 4 to 6 p.m.

Morning Dress, Uniform or Lounge Suit

From very small numbers Dimensions was soon working with over 600 young people in years 9, 10 and 11 in around 50 schools across Yorkshire. Four years later Dimensions now has 6 Hairdressing Academies in

Top: Bill and Bernadette at the Henley Regatta. Left: A very proud moment for Bill and Bernadette was the invitation (inset) to a Garden Party at Buckingham Palace in July, 1991. Below: Bill with Ray Roberts MBE in the Cash & Carry at Meadowhall.

schools - in Barnsley, Batley, Wakefield, Leeds and Northallerton and plans to open another 10 in the near future. In addition to these, the company has City Centre Hairdressing Academies in Barnsley, Sheffield, Wakefield and Leeds and Beauty Academies, a new venture for the business, in Barnsley and Northallerton with additional ones planned soon

Dimensions today is truly a family affair with Bill and Bernadette being joined in the business by Tina Shaw, their daughter, a director of the company who also qualified as a hairdresser in the early 1990s. Tina is now responsible for the day-to-day running of the original salon in Peel St Arcade, in Barnsley, and is now assisted by her daughter Brittany, who is the third generation to work in the family business and is a product of the Dimensions Training Academy.

The group Director of Finance (and Bill's PA), Patricia Stevenson, is Bernadette's sister and Carl, Bill and Bernadette's son, also a hairdresser, has three salons in the Wakefield area and works on a consultancy basis carrying out demonstrations for the training division. When not thinking about business - those who know Bill well would say "it just doesn't happen" - Bill has a passion for football, and in particular Barnsley Football Club. One of Bill's proudest moments was seeing the corner stand at Oakwell become 'The Dimensions Stand' emblazoned with the company's logo and the slogan 'Football and fashion are always a passion at Dimensions'.

Today, turnover is rapidly approaching the £2 million mark, with plans for much more growth. Bill is also a Council Member of the Hairdressing Council, the regulatory body for hairdressers in the UK and was Chairman of the Council, which meets in London, for 3 years before taking over as Treasurer, a position he still holds.

When asked why he thought he and Dimensions had become so successful Bill says "Not wishing to sound like a walking cliché, but Vidal Sassoon, who is probably the best known hairdresser in the world, once said 'the only place you find success before work, is in the dictionary'!"

"Without doubt, the main reason for my success is the people I've been fortunate enough to know and work with. Starting with my father - who was more than a dad to me, he was my hero. Jon Major was a great partner and it seems unbelievable that it's more than two decades ago since we went our separate ways. Ray Roberts MBE, who, other than my father, taught me more about business than anyone else and was there to support Bernadette and myself when we needed it."

"Last, but by no means least, for the last 30 plus years, Bernadette has supported me throughout in both the good and not so good times and, along with my family, continues to inspire and motivate me to go on."

*Far left: Dimensions Batley. **Left:** Dimensions 2009/10 prospectus. **Above:** The Dimensions Stand' with the slogan 'Football and Fashion are always a Passion at Dimensions'. **Below:** Back (L to R) Carl Shaw and Bill Shaw, front (L to R) Brittany Wollerton, Bernadette Shaw, Patricia Stevenson and Tina Shaw.*

The Rack Group
From Market Trader to Market Leader

The Rack Group Ltd, based in Shawfield Road, on the Carlton Industrial Estate, near Barnsley, has grown remarkably over the course of its existence.

Pallet racking is one of the least glamorous yet vitally important parts of commerce. Without high-rise racking systems warehouses would occupy many times more space than they do – and warehousing would cost much more, a price ultimately paid by everyone.

The correct installation of storage equipment is absolutely critical for a smooth running and safe warehouse. In an industry where rogue installation companies are rife, The Rack Group prides itself on having a reputation as the best. Formerly a Dexion installation company. The Rack Group is now one of only a few remaining 'apprentice trained' installation companies.

The Rack Group has a strict, trained and competent group of installers with an excellent, proven, history in installation capabilities and interaction with customers. Installers are expected to be ambassadors and to perform with courtesy and respect for customers. They arrive with the philosophy that they are there to compliment a client's business, not to disrupt it.

Experienced and capable of handling all types of material and equipment to meet all HSE requirements as a basic minimum, the group provides all of its installers with specific guidelines, installation directions and drawings. The Rack Group has an experienced supervisor on each project. On large projects it appoints a senior manager to start the job and make sure everything begins on time, runs without foreseeable problems and sees the job to a successful completion.

Clients range from small business to FTSE and Fortune 500 companies. Individual client relationships are essential to success and the group has repeatedly proven to them that its goal is to satisfy their needs. Clients want the best and The Rack Group are the experts for warehouse layout, design and material handling equipment.

The Rack Group story began in the early 1970s when two young men, Phil Smith and Len Batty, found themselves married to two sisters and both with two young families to feed. Although the two young men were fully employed they felt the urgent need to do more to provide for their growing families. It didn't take them long to start selling together on weekend markets; their stock

Top: Co-founders Phil Smith and Len Batty. **Left and above:** Phil (third from right) and the lads take a well-earned break while installing racking for Mars, in Swindon, in the company's early years.

delivering to being closed because of the three day week which had been introduced to conserve national fuel stocks.

Inevitably the transport business did not last long. Brian Bellwood, who had previously been an ambulance driver, eventually returned to driving ambulances. Len Batty, however, stayed with the company until 1999.

In the mid-1970s whilst looking for other opportunities to earn a wage doing something new Len saw an advert for Pallet Racking installers in a newspaper for a company called Dexion Ltd which was a manufacturer of storage equipment. This is where the racking connection all began.

varied from washing machines to records and ladies underwear, to name but a few of the many and varied products they sold.

After a while the pair of young entrepreneurs decided they should take matters a step further. After their first attempt to branch out and work for themselves, they started a transport/delivery company. Len's half brother Brian Bellwood joined them and BSB Transport (Batty, Smith and Bellwood) was set up. Unfortunately for the trio, serious problems lay ahead. Not long after starting the business a fuel and power shortage took place and many companies had to revert to a three day week. How could three lads from Wakefield have anticipated events on the world stage? In October, 1973, the Arab-Israeli War broke out. In reaction OPEC announced that it would reduce oil production until Israel withdrew from the territories it had occupied.

The consequence of OPEC's actions were felt everywhere. Britain barely avoided the introduction of petrol rationing. The UK economy teetered on the edge of a precipice. And for transport firms that meant double trouble. Phil remembers having to carry extra fuel around in the back of the wagon to ensure he got back home as they often found themselves going to a petrol station to fill up and found that it was either closed or that there was no fuel. Also on many occasions they could not hand over their loads due to the companies they were

In 1982, after having worked as a partnership, the team decided to set up three limited companies: BSB Erections, BSB Developments and BSB Holdings. Phil, Len and numerous family members worked installing pallet racking for a number of years.

Over the years the business made many investments both on a personal level and through the company. One of the early investments was a public house which was bought to re-develop it. The pub was called the Milton Arms and was located in Hemingfield. After almost two years of renovating the pub was re-opened as the Fiddlers Inn and was very popular for many years with the local community.

— FIDDLERS INN —

Top: John Smith Engineers yard Left: The renovated Fiddlers Inn.

In 1997 the whole group was re-structured and Phil became the Managing Director. Long standing employees Vicki Sugden, Jenny Charlton, Scott Maxwell-Smith and Simon Lee were invited to join the board of directors and later became shareholders. The new board of directors made a positive decision to move away from working for the manufacturers. They decided it was time to have more control of the business; this meant taking a positive attitude to working for the end users.

After a time some of the family members left to pursue other interests. Slowly, however, the company grew and BSB Erections employed more and more installers; at one period it employed 100 staff made up of direct labour and sub-contractors.

Meanwhile, in 1987, BSB Developments had invested in an existing engineering company called John Smith Engineers, a business established in 1864. BSB inherited many old artefacts and memorabilia along with pictures of the early workforce at John Smith's. Vic Lawrence was retained to run the engineering business. Vic was a time served apprentice and started working at Smith's at the age of 15.

Installation jobs covered the whole of the UK, but after a call to the company from Holland in 1992 the company branched out into mainland Europe. Holland and Germany became one of the more lucrative markets and the company was employed on a number of European projects when the exchange rates were in favour, making UK labour more cost effective than continental workers.

In the meantime Phil's family changed their name to Maxwell-Smith in memory of a special nephew, Maxwell.

The company had previously carried out racking safety inspections for some blue chip companies such as ASDA and Britvic Soft Drinks. It was decided the racking safety inspections was one of the directions that would help grow the company and this proved to be successful. The company moved premises to Carlton Industrial Estate to accommodate the changes which began to take place in the company.

Top left: Pictured outside John Smith Engineers in 2002 are from left to right: Alison Horbury Vicki Sugden and Jenny Charlton, picture insert Vic on the right in his teens. **Above:** Vic Lawrence and Corrine Maxwell-Smith at Vic's retirement in October, 1997. **Below:** BSB Erections on their way to a job in East Germany. **Below left:** Working on a site in East Germany.

Since then the company has not looked back, inspections are growing at a steady rate and it now inspects over 500 different sites each year.

In fact the timing of the change could not have been better. Health and Safety in the UK became a top priority throughout industry in general, and having to provide a safer environment for workers in warehouse situations was, and is, a paramount objective.

Meanwhile, after some serious thought and deliberations, Phil decided that a name change was necessary to rebrand the company and give it an image more descriptive of its actual function and no longer about individual names. And so 'The Rack Group' was born. Today the group incorporates a total of five rack-related limited companies: Rack Management Ltd, The Rack Group Ltd, Rack Armour Ltd, Rack Training Ltd and Rent a Rack Ltd.

Taken together the combined companies form what the group calls the 'Rack Aid Package' and covers every aspect of total rack care. Many blue chip companies now benefit from the services, products, specialist equipment and training that the Rack Aid Package offers. This Rack Aid Package is unique with patented and design registered products.

Not only does the Rack Aid Package simplify the inspection, maintenance and protection of pallet racking it can also reduce the costs of ownership by thousands of pounds in any one year. The group has saved one of its largest blue chip companies over one million pounds in repair costs.

The company has developed and patented a new product to reduce damage to pallet racking called Rack Armour, which is probably the best pallet racking protector in the world. The company has distributors in America, Canada, Mexico, Chile, Iceland, France, Belgium, Netherlands, Germany, Taiwan, Australia, Israel, Romania, Egypt, Ireland and Portugal.

Above left: Racking with Rack Armour, probably the best pallet racking protector in the world, fitted. Below: Shelley Maxwell-Smith, daughter of Phil, and Alex Robinson, of Rack Armour Australia, at an exhibition in Sydney. Bottom left: The company's stand at the exhibition. Bottom right: Phil Maxwell-Smith bumps into Aussie cricketing legend Dennis Lillee at the exhibition.

The company manufactures the guard in Tipton, Birmingham, Erie, Pennsylvania USA, and Sydney, Australia. The products are supplied to many household and High Street names including Disney World, Ikea, Caterpillar, Sainsburys, DHL, Asda, Laura Ashley, Johnson & Johnson, Marks & Spencer, Tesco and Argos.

Rack Training enables warehouse staff to recognise damaged racking and what the implications can be to their organisation, to identify what damage needs urgent repair and which damage is less of a danger. This helps warehouse managers tremendously. The company has also tried to raise the standards and working conditions for installers within the industry, and with this in mind one of the Directors, Simon Lee, has worked to develop an NVQ for pallet racking installation. He has been very successful in that project, and with the aid of a working group the NVQ is now in use.

The Group also offers clients the facility of renting racking over the periods when they get exceptionally busy, at Christmas time for example. This helps businesses spread the cost, plus there are definite tax advantages for short term rental against buying pallet racking. Many companies have taken up on this facility and return every year, for example Marks & Spencer rents racking for storing turkeys at Christmas.

Down the years The Rack Group has developed specialist equipment and gained design rights for them. One of the designs is a lifting jack or SLP (Sacrificial Leg Prop) as it is known. This removes the need to offload racking whilst it is being repaired and facilitates the fitting of specially designed repair legs.

As a forward thinking company The Rack Group encourages its employees to use their initiative and come up with ideas for improvements. Over the years the group has won a number of business awards in recognition of its achievements in various fields.

The group regularly exhibits its products and services in the UK and overseas. It has exhibited in Chicago, Illinois, Cleveland, Ohio, and Sydney, Australia. Its distributors have also exhibited its products in France and Germany.

Top right: *Phil Maxwell-Smith signs up a Rent-A-Rack truck.* ***Above left:*** *left to right: Simon Lee, Chris Chan, Kevin Chan, Vicki Sugden, Tim Smith and Jenny Charlton pictured at a training session for Chris and Kevin from Rack Armour Distributors in Taiwan.* ***Below left:*** *Phil Maxwell-Smith pictured with son Scott Maxwell-Smith, Director (right), and Installations Manager Richard Lee (left) at the Wakefield Hospice Charity Ball.* ***Below:*** *Wombwell Warriors Under-11 football team sponsored by the Rack Group.*

Encouraging sporting activities is part of The Rack Group philosophy and the group regularly sponsors a number of teams along with individuals. Beneficiaries include Wombwell Warriors Under-11 football team (which won their league in 2009) and the British Lions Great Britain Rugby League under-23s, which had a very successful tour in Ukraine in 2009. In recognition of his talent a member of the British Lions team, Zack Johnson, has been approached by a number of professional rugby clubs. Zack is Phil's nephew and Phil is very proud of his sporting achievements.

Ideally located at the centre of mainland Great Britain, The Rack Group is a purveyor of the common Yorkshire values of honesty, fairness, grit and pride in what it can do and the quality of its works. The Rack Group Ltd is a strong, inclusive and loyal family that draws from the best traditions of seeing 'a good job done'.

With dozens of years of experience in the business the group has found success in its ability to provide quality products and services to any size of customer. The customer base ranges from FTSE 100 and Fortune 500 conglomerates to small medium sizes in every county in the U.K. The Rack Group is a proactive member of the Royal Society for the Prevention of Accidents (RoSPA) and the Institute of Occupations Safety and Health (IOSH); it is also the only storage equipment servicing company to currently hold the government's Contractors Health and Safety Evaluation Scheme (CHAS).

The path from market trader to market leader has taken many twists and turns down the decades. Today however everyone who has ever been involved with The Rack Group over the years can take pride in the knowledge that each of them has played a part in the creation of a business that not only Barnsley, but the whole of Britain, can take pride in.

Top left: The under 23 Great Britain rugby league team, sponsored by the Rack Group, on their successful tour of the Ukraine. Inset is team member Zack Johnson, nephew of Phil Maxwell-Smith. **Below:** *The Rack Group Directors, from left to right: Simon Lee, Vicki Sugden, Phil Maxwell-Smith, Jenny Charlton and Scott Maxwell-Smith.* **Bottom:** *The Rack Group, Carlton Industrial Estate, Barnsley.*

Jakto - Moving the Earth

Jakto Transport Ltd, now based in Oaks Lane, Stairfoot, in Barnsley, is the area's number one firm when it comes to Bulk Earthworks, Site Clearance, Demolition, Remediation, Civil Engineering and Road Haulage projects. The company has vast knowledge and over 40 years of experience in the construction industry, with 90% of its growth being as a result of client recommendations.

Noted for being honest, trustworthy and completely committed to customer satisfaction, the company may be based in Barnsley but many of its recent projects have taken its staff all across the country. Jakto employs over 100 personnel. The firm takes care of highways projects from 'Concept to Completion' covering road and dual carriageway construction, road surfacing/re-surfacing, and road maintenance. Staff plan and carry out all the major constituents of highways schemes in-house so that clients can be assured that their projects will always be properly managed, completed on time and within budget.

Jakto regularly wins contracts from local authority and national highways bodies, including some on a quality selection basis, making it one of the largest road construction contractors/specialists in the Midlands and North of England. As clients move away from traditional tendering techniques, the firm now routinely take part in the latest procurement methods, including partnering.

From challenging emergency rock cutting remedial works – finished ahead of schedule – to the pre-programmed resurfacing of major highways, Jakto staff have experience in planning complex traffic management arrangements, safely ensuring minimal disruption to the travelling public.

The current company owes its existence to George Hellewell who in 1955 started out in business as a haulage contractor. It was in 1964 that George's son, Tony Hellewell, the present Managing Director, and his wife, Jackie, set up their own company, Jakto Transport Ltd, to concentrate on bulk haulage. The name of the company is a combination of the original directors' names.

The original business was based around coal haulage, moving coal around the extensive coalfields of South Yorkshire. With the demise of the coal industry, however, it was essential for the company to diversify its operations and so in the early 1990s Jakto started to move into the bulk excavation market.

That move was the catalyst for continuous expansion and improvement with the Company working closely with Major Contractors to develop that growth.

One example of the company's ability to react quickly was the Sutton Landfill site for waste in Nottinghamshire. Within 48 hours Jakto had prepared a contract and commenced working on site. The contract, which consisted of preparation works for a new landfill cell ,involved a cut and fill operation of 420,000 tonnes in six weeks or approximately 11,000 tonnes per day. Despite bad weather the contract was completed to schedule.

One of the main areas of Jakto's expertise is land reclamation. In 1995 Jakto carried out the reclamation of

Top: Founders Tony and Jackie Hellewell. **Left:** George Hellewell, Tony's father alongside the company's first vehicle, who inspired Tony and Jackie to set up their own transport company.

Donisthorpe Colliery for Leicester County Council, converting a derelict site into a part of the National Forest. This involved the reshaping of over 30 hectares of land by moving 200,000 tonnes of spoil, the excavation of a canal, replacing the towpaths, and constructing a number of new cycle paths together with brick feature bridges spanning existing water courses. The contract had a value of £1.6 million.

Other major contracts carried out included, in 1994, enabling works for a new cargo apron at East Midlands Airport. In seven weeks 80,000 tonnes of material were excavated and removed from site to tip and a hard standing formed of imported Type One Sub-base, a quarried material.

Also in 1994, but much nearer to home, Jakto carried out a tip capping operation at Cudworth North Junction Landfill, Barnsley. That work consisted of reshaping the surface of the tip, capping it with 100,000 tonnes of special clay incorporating a geotextile membrane and laying a layer of subsoil for tree planting.

Another local contract involved the development of the Old Moor and Wetland Reserve for Rotherham Borough Council. This was an interesting job involving the construction of concrete roads, the building of the reserve, including shallow ponds and islands, and the construction of hides for bird watchers.

A potentially hazardous contract involved the removal of 240,000 tonnes of heavily contaminated material resulting from the reclamation of Stanton Iron and Gas Works, at Ilkeston. The material resulting from a cut and fill operation was transported to a special tip 44 miles away. The contract also involved road construction and was valued at £1.8 million.

Another large contract was for Rotherham Borough Council with a value of £2.3 million. This involved the reclamation of 37 hectares of derelict land. Some 600,000 tonnes of slag were excavated from the site and processed as aggregates for the construction industry. The site was brought up to level with 500,000 tonnes of imported fill and compacted ready for the developers to begin construction of industrial units. The contract was completed in 12 months.

Top: Work in progress at Temple Sowerby by-pass in 2007.
Left: Screening excavated material for re-use. ***Below:*** *A Jakto crusher in operation producing usable aggregates from construction waste.*

Recent projects have included the £10 million M1 widening at J25-26 Nottingham, the £5 million contract for the Hemsworth Bypass/A1 Link, the East Midlands Distribution Centre, Castle Donnington - Earthworks costing £1.5million, Markham Grange Reclamation, and million-pound enabling works at York University.

Jakto has developed into one of the premier remediation contractors in Yorkshire. With government pressure to utilise Brownfield Sites and the increased costs associated with disposing of contaminated materials, the business has evolved to provide solutions to differing customer requirements.

Although based in Barnsley, Jakto has worked on contracts all over the United Kingdom, for example preparing the groundwork for a £5 million salmon processing factory on the Scottish Borders.

The company's annual turnover doubled yearly during the 1990s and now stands at £20 million. This was achieved when many similar companies failed, and is a tribute to the strength and character of the company and its employees. That progress can be also attributed in part to a strategy which includes providing the complete package of reclamation, groundworks, drainage and infrastructure.

The groundworks and drainage division can, and does ,operate independently. Substructure and external works packages were completed on retail parks in Wakefield and Huddersfield. Working in conjunction with the excavation section, large diameter surface water drainage was installed at Harrogate Hydro. Other work included the construction of a large in situ concrete culvert for the Wath Manvers spine road in Rotherham, and precast concrete box culverts on sites in Wakefield and Sheffield.

The company is able to provide a dedicated Bulk Earthworks and materials re-engineering service. As a specialist contractor it is able to add expertise from the years of experience it has gained along with wide experience of significant Civil Engineering schemes.

Jakto also undertakes all types of demolition from major industrial projects to localised dismantling. All projects are staffed by fully trained and certified personnel who work within the company's Zero Risk policy. Jakto is experienced in dealing with all relevant bodies to ensure compliance with current legislation and can offer a service which takes over responsibility for the demolition on a project from concept to completion.

Top left. Bulk excavation and groundworks by Jakto. **Left:** *Jakto operate a fleet of eight wheeled tipper lorries catering for any type of bulk materials.* **Above:** *A wide range of plant hire equipment is available for long or short term hire from Jakto.*

for vehicle and plant maintenance as well as storage areas for mobile plant. Attached to the yard is the licensed transfer station allowing Jakto to take full advantage of recycling opportunities. The company is proud to boast that it recycles 100% of materials that enter the site.

As for the future, Jakto is perfectly positioned to take full advantage of every chance to progress – and to evolve to meet new needs as they arise.

After more than forty years in the business this family firm has never yet failed to turn challenges into opportunities, and it aims to make sure it continues to do so in the years ahead.

Meanwhile, Jakto Haulage still offers the exceptional service in haulage it has been providing since the 1960s. The company's comprehensive fleet of tipper trucks are self-sheeting, equipped with on board weighers and operate under Jakto's waste carriers' licence at its 11 acre Licensed Transfer Station, in Barnsley.

Top left. The company has the capacity to carry out all types of demolition and industrial foundation removal. *Left:* Groundworks. *Above:* The Hellewell family; Jackie and Tony (front) and son Adrian (back left), daughter Sarah (back centre) and son Neil (back right). *Below:* A bird's eye view of the Jakto premises, Oaks Lane, Stairfoot, Barnsley, 2010.

Although the company has seen dramatic expansion over the years and has developed into one of the most respected companies in the North of England it is still very much a family firm with Neil, Sarah and Adrian Hellewell joining the Board of Directors.

The company is based adjacent to Oaks Business Park, Barnsley, which is ideally situated for the main conurbations of South and West Yorkshire together with easy access to the major motorway networks, allowing greater flexibility for the large fleet of tipper lorries and other plant. The depot has facilities

C. Soar & Sons - Transforming Business

C. Soar & Sons, formed in 1956, is the leading electrical equipment dismantling company in the UK. In the process of achieving that eminent status the company has also become one of Britain's most environmentally conscious and responsible businesses.

As the UK's largest purchaser of used transformers and electrical plant for recycling C. Soar and Sons has an enviable reputation for reliability and professionalism. Its commitment to providing a comprehensive ethical disposal service, which satisfies all health and safety and environmental demands has gained the company a unique reputation within its industry.

The company was founded by Clarence Soar as a general scrap merchant but he soon specialised into working with scrap cable and dismantling electrical equipment left over from the Second World War and from the mining industry. This eventually evolved into working with regional electrical companies and power stations.

Yet few would have predicted the company's founder would one day find himself at the head of a thriving business. The last born of a very large mining family, Clarence Soar, was born with a disability which meant undergoing many operations on his feet and legs when he was a small child.

These medical procedures were paid for by the chapel since the cost was far beyond his father's means, in those days long before the National Health Service came into existence.

With the more usual boyish pursuits denied to him, Clarence spent part of his boyhood learning to play the piano, something which his disability did not prevent, and a possible way for him to one day earn his living.

During the Second World War Clarence's disability exempted him from National Service. Instead, during the hostilities, he earned a living as maintenance fitter for a glass bottle manufacturer.

*Top left. Founder, Clarence Soar. **Above:** Clarence and his wife taking a trip on the 'Norwich Belle' at Yarmouth. **Below:** A 1970s view of the site at Old Tank Row.*

unwanted shelters and sell them for scrap. He tried his hand at cable stripping, too, recovering the copper from old electrical cables. This was eventually followed by buying and dismantling old electrical transformers which contained vastly larger quantities of valuable metal. In 1956, Clarence set up his own firm in Old Tank Row, Stairfoot, Barnsley.

Born into a large family, Clarence would have a large family himself: four daughters and four sons. The boys joined him in the business as each of them left school. When Clarence died in 1990 at the age of 71 the three of his sons who were by now partners, David, Colin and Michael, took over the business. A fourth brother, Brian, had left the firm not long before their father's death.

When the former bottle factory workers were demobilised from the armed forces at the end of the war and returned to their jobs there was no more work for Clarence at the factory.

Hard times however, make hard men. Clarence had no intention of just sitting at home and expecting the more able-bodied members of his family to provide for him. Now he decided to turn his early music lessons to account by earning a living as a piano tuner.

Yet Clarence was nothing if not versatile, and piano tuning was not a major-money spinner; he further augmented his income by, at various times, making artificial Christmas trees, manufacturing pushchairs, and selling crockery on Barnsley market.

Clarence also noticed that the end of the war had brought with it an unexpected business opportunity. During the war thousands of corrugated iron Anderson air raid shelters had been built in gardens. Clarence began to buy the now

The first major problem the three brothers had to face was the introduction of the Environmental Protection Act. As a result of that new legislation the brothers had to choose between closing the business or now investing heavily in new equipment to comply with the new law. They chose the latter course and acquired the Vernon Works in 1993. Whilst this was gutted and re-equipped to meet the new regulations work at Tank Row continued.

An unequivocal commitment to environmental protection has since ensured the company's place as the contractor of choice for its many clients.

In 1995, more land and office building were acquired. The offices were re-equipped and decorated whilst new warehouses were built alongside them.

Top left. A 1980s bird's eye view of Tank Row works. **Below:** *The Tank Row offices after refurbishment in 1997.*

Fortunately the demand for the services of C. Soar and Sons grew as the modernisation programme progressed; as a result the fresh investment quickly began to pay for itself.

Many new types of waste, including transformer oil and transformer cores impregnated with oil, have now been classified as hazardous waste. Oil is a highly visible form of pollution. It harms plants and animals, damages rivers, groundwater and the soil and can destroy natural habitats and drinking water supplies. It is the most commonly reported type of water pollution.

In response to that challenge C. Soar & Sons aims to be the best and most environmentally friendly operator in the industry – to be nothing less than a centre of excellence in its chosen field. The company's facilities are specially designed and built to prevent contamination. Fully concreted yards with complete perimeter 'bund' walls and high risk 'bund' areas means there is no possibility of leakage into ground or water courses. Rainwater is captured

by interceptor tanks and separated so that only clean water is discharged into drains. The company also has the facilities to remove, store and process 160,000 litres of insulating oil. All tanks are regularly inspected by the Environment Agency.

The company is one of only a handful in the United Kingdom approved and authorised as a bonded oil distributor, and is allowed to export redundant equipment to China and the Far East.

Long term contracts were won with most of the regional electrical companies such as Scottish and Southern Energy, EDF Energy Networks, United Utilities, Scottish Power and CE Electric.

By-products of the dismantling of transformers were sold to such companies as could make use of them: copper manufacturers, the oil industry and scrap metal dealers. Core steel was sold to the Middle and Far East for restamping.

The company has the most comprehensive and up-to-date waste management licence in the industry. Each year the business collects more than 8,000 tonnes of redundant electrical equipment, of which some 98% is recovered and recycled. No other operator in the industry is able to boast such an impressive recycling rate.

Over the years the company has dealt with every shape and size of electrical plant, and has dismantled transformers ranging from just 50kg up to 670 tonnes.

Inevitably such activity requires a lot of moving equipment. The firm has a fleet of flat

Today the business remains entirely in private ownership and is now run by the two remaining partners Colin and Michael Soar, the second and third generations of the Soar family. With over 40 employees C. Soar & Sons may have now become a global business, but it remains very proud of its roots in Barnsley, and of the remarkable enterprise shown by its founder, Clarence Soar.

As for the future, in their own words: "We wish to build on our reputation by becoming recognised as the centre of expertise in the disposal of power transformers. We are a company which can be trusted to operate in an ethical and responsible manner, safeguarding the environment and the well being of our employees and those of our clients in contact with our activities. In doing this we wish to make a fair profit and develop our business in areas where we can use our skills positively."

bed trailers; four tractor units with 40 tonne lorry-mounted cranes. Another tractor unit is fitted with a 65 tonne lorry-mounted crane for heavier equipment. Two 32 tonne roll-on roll-off skip wagons compete with numerous skips have been specifically designed and built for transporting electrical equipment.

In keeping with a commitment to caring for the environment the entire fleet of HGVs have reduced pollution certificates and Euro 3/4/5 engines to minimise their impact on the environment. The company has calculated that by using such environmentally friendly vehicles it has reduced its carbon footprint to that of a small mini-cab business operating in the local area.

As for safety, the company has had no major incidents in over 50 years. Its safety record is exemplary, working in some of the biggest power stations in the country, including Sizewell, Fiddlers Ferry, Hinkley Point and Ferrybridge, as well as at its own site.

Meanwhile investment continues. A new 8-acre site in Rotherham is in the process at a cost of £7 million.

David Soar left the company in 2002.

Facing page and above: At work with C. Soar & Sons. The company's processes are carried out in line with current environmental legislation. With the lowest score rating in their industry, the rigorous managements systems the company have in place are easy to see. *Below:* An aerial view of Tank Row in 2010.

Ron Daley - A Winner On Two Wheels

Today, based at 46-52 Doncaster Road, Barnsley, Ron Daley Scooters is one of Barnsley's best known business names. Established in 1958, the firm has over 50 years experience as a two-wheel specialist and it boasts one of the largest stocks of new and used scooters in the UK.

A full range of all the current franchises is always kept in stock, all the way from 50cc mopeds and 500cc touring and sports scooters, to race replica geared bikes, and of course traditional and automatic Vespa scooters.

Personal recommendation and repeat business are a big part of new sales, and that can only be achieved by looking after customers. It's not only sales that count; repairs and service work remain as important a part of the business, just as they did back in 1958 when the firm was founded.

Ron Daley's may want to sell customers a scooter, but, unlike some dealers, the firm sees that as just the beginning. Whether a bike is for work or for pleasure, experienced staff are there to ensure every bike gives years of trouble-free service.

Well known local figure Ronald Daley started repairing cycles and motorcycles in 1946 whilst still at school.

In 1947 Ron left school at the age of 14 and started work as an apprentice joiner in the building trade. His wage was just 6p an hour, £1.46 per week. He did two nights at the technical college, one night studying building construction and one night studying motor engineering.

Meanwhile in his spare time Ron did motorcycle repairs in a converted greenhouse, a makeshift 'workshop' located in the back garden of his parents' council prefab home.

Completing his apprenticeship in 1954, Ron got a job in the joiners shop at the local colliery, the hours were 6am to 2.50pm. That same year he joined the Barnsley Motorcycle and Car Club; he bought an old DOT trials bike which he used for trials, grass tracking, scrambling and, of course, transport to and from work.

After winning the 1955-56 Club championship a club member suggested Ron went on a blind date with Marian, a friend of his, taking her to the club dinner dance and prize giving. There Ron would receive no fewer than seven trophies for his successes during the year.

Ron found out later that Marian had a motorcycle and

Top: *Ron and Marian Daley in 1958.* **Left and bottom left:** *Ron winning Pillion Trials in 1955 and scrambling in 1954.* **Below:** *Where it all began, the converted greenhouse used by Ron as a makeshift workshop.*

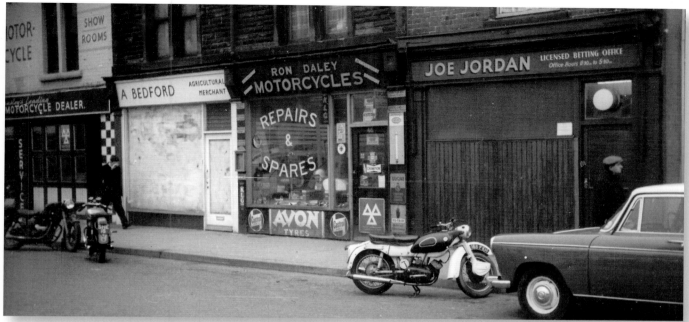

a full motorcycle license, something which was rather unusual in the nineteen fifties.

Marion and Ron were clearly made for each other.

In August, 1958, Marian and Ron were married. They bought a house for £150 and rented a nearby stable for a workshop at 4s/6d per week. There Ron started his motorcycle business. After refurbishing their house it was sold in 1960 in order to buy a shop at 46, Doncaster Road. The basement was fitted out as a workshop, the first floor as a showroom and the second floor and attic as a flat which Ron and Marian now moved into. In order to accumulate some capital, however, Ron would carry on working at the pit for another five years: he was up at 5am for the pit. Marian opened the shop in the morning until Ron came home at 3pm and worked in the workshop until 10 or 11 in the evening.

Ron and Marian's first son, Martin, was born on 27 April, 1961. A year later Ron finished building an extension at the rear of the shop with an MOT test bay for testing motorcycles.

A second son, Philip, was born in December, 1963.

That same year Ron finished working at the colliery and bought an old BSA A10 650cc for £12 to which was fitted a chassis and a large box sidecar; this was the means of collecting broken down motorcycles and other transport duties.

The business was now growing. By 1964 Ron had to employ another mechanic to keep pace with demand. More space too was needed, and in 1965 the Daley family moved out from living above the shop into a new bungalow. Two years later a third son, Christopher, arrived.

The demand for scooters grew throughout the 1960s and in 1967 Ron Daley took over the Vespa franchise from the previous dealership. The firm sold many Vespa scooters and accessories. The next year the Yamaha franchise was also acquired and business boomed: Yamaha's FS1E moped, DT125 and the RS100 sold in large quantities.

*Top: The first shop, 46 Doncaster Road. **Above left:** Martin Daley outside the shop in the 1960s. **Below:** Young Philip Daley on the works transport in 1967.*

With work increasing daily, Ron's brother in law, Donald Nixon, started work in the shop in 1970. Two years later the betting shop next door came up for sale and was snapped up by Ron. The party wall was taken out, doubling the size of the shop.

The business officially became a limited company in 1973 as Ron Daley Motorcycles Ltd, with Ron himself as the Managing Director and Marian as Company Secretary.

Further expansion came in 1975 when the double shop premises next door came up for sale. More party walls were removed to double the size of the premises yet again.

Sons Martin and Philip began working with their father in their spare time as soon as they were able. In 1977 at the age of 16 Martin became a full time employee. Two years later, once he had reached 16, his younger brother Philip also joined the family firm.

The 1980s would usher in a period of ever-increasing business. In 1984 the company took over the Reliant franchise from the previous dealer. This would prove to be a real money spinner as both new and used Reliants sold brilliantly.

Third son Christopher Daley began work at the shop aged 18 in 1985. That same year a new MOT bay was built where cars and three wheelers could be tested.

Suzuki took over importing Vespa in 1985, however, it imported very few spares or machines and as a result Ron Daley terminated the franchise. The Yamaha franchise would eventually end too. In 1991 the company finally stopped selling Yamahas because in 1977 the transport minister had banned the top selling model, the FSIE moped, and changed the driving licensing laws on some of the other models, this eventually wrecked Yamaha sales.

Something new was needed to fill the gap. In 1994 the firm took on the Lada franchise. There was a loyal following for Lada, true they had their problems, but the warranty system was good and it kept the workshops busy.

Three years later, however, things began to unravel. Reliant went bankrupt, and equally badly, Lada could not meet new emission rules - that was the end of Lada in the United Kingdom. Things looked very bleak indeed for the family firm: no Ladas, no Reliants, no Yamahas and no Vespas, just an empty showroom apart from a few used machines.

It was then that Martin Daley had the feeling there was going to be another scooter boom, just like in the sixties. It turned out he was right! Piaggio had started importing its own excellent scooter range, which included the Vespa.

Ron Daley Motorcycles Ltd now applied for the Piaggio franchise and got it. Today the company has a showroom packed with scooters and sells them all over the country. There is a high demand for Martin's special editions. The firm also now has a busy mail ordering business, sending items all over the world.

Above: *Advertising from the late 1960s and early 1970s.* **Bottom left:** *Bikes ready on the trailer for competition in the early days.* **Below:** *Ron and sons Martin, Philip and Christopher out scrambling in April, 1976.*

sales, used machine purchasing and counter sales. Donald Nixon is now Showroom Manager, Machine Sales and Finance. Philip Daley takes care of collections, deliveries, counter sales and mail order whilst Sam Daley is Web Development Manager as well as counter sales and mail order.

With business booming once again Ron and Marian's grandson, Sam, joined the firm aged 18 in 2007 following the now traditional experience of working part-time. Ron Daley remains Managing Director in charge of stock control and paying bills and Marian Daley is still Company Secretary. In the workshops Martin Daley is Workshop Manager with a particular responsibility for special editions as designer/builder, repairs, Vespa PX models and vintage scooters.

Scott Littlewood is 'Wheels to Work' Manager and automatic scooter specialist. Darren Kilgarriff does general scooter repairs, tyre fitting, motorcycle MOTs, whilst Simon Horn is MOT tester and Test Bay Manager.

Elsewhere Christopher Daley is General Manager in charge of advertising, accounts and spares, and Scott Oxley is Parts Manager taking care of vehicle

The firm is certainly set to keep the wheels turning for many more years to come.

Top left and inset *Taking delivery of scooters and a scooter rally meeting outside Ron Daley's.* ***Left:*** *Ron and Marian pictured in 2007.* ***Above:*** *Marian and Ron pictured with sons Philip, Chris and Martin.* ***Below:*** *The Ron Daley 46-52 Doncaster Road premises in 2010.*

Barnsley Market - the Heart of the Town

There is an old saying - "If they dun't sell it on Barnsley Market, they dun't mek it!" Perhaps not entirely accurate, but close enough to the truth.

Even before the Norman Conquest of 1066 people were bringing goods to sell at a market in the small town of Barnsley. Later a system of granting Royal Charters was devised by the Norman kings, allowing markets to be held only in certain towns. Barnsley was granted a market charter in February 1249 under the auspices of Pontefract monastery. Following the dissolution of the monasteries in the 16th century, the charter reverted first to the Crown, and then through the years was devolved into the hands of Barnsley MBC.

Barnsley Market thrived. The market place however, was used for more than just selling goods and produce. In 1405 it was decreed that stocks be set up in every town: in Barnsley stocks were erected on Market Hill adjoining the Market and the Moot (meeting) Hall. In the 18th century floggings were also carried out there.

The Market Place was always considered the centre of the town where its citizens would gather, being for centuries located at the top of Market Hill and Churchfields close to St. Mary's church and the Moot Hall.

The Moot Hall served various functions – court Quarter Sessions were held there from the 14th until the 19th century. Market stalls were once stored in the basement.

The area was also a place where people gathered for celebrations. Through the centuries however, the market has altered its position several times, whilst always remaining the heart of the town.

Due to religious objections that it was too close to the church the market moved downhill to Market Hill. By 1825 it became clear that the site was too small to hold all the would-be traders and the market expanded into May Day Green. Peel Square was also used at one time.

In the 1930s a new market was established south of Queens Market and east of May Day Green.

In 1939 the Queens Market was dug up and a labyrinth of air raid shelters built undergound. Though sealed off after the war they remained there until a new market was built in the 1970s.

kept safe in the hopes of its one day being placed in a prominent position in a new market.

Down the decades the market has had its troubles. On 14th June, 1969, there was a sudden rainstorm which flooded the market. Some traders who stacked their goods on the floor saw their stock being washed away. In the Gas Nook the water rose so high that it raised the boards of the stalls, and the goods upon them which were similarly lost.

Market trading was not usually so hazardous, and from the 1930s to 1970s the market was so full that traders were often hard pressed to find a vacant stall.

From Victorian times the market had continued to grow, until in the 1970s it occupied a considerable area around Market Hill, Mayday Green and the 'Gas Nook'. For most of that period there was also a livestock market where horses, sheep and cattle were traded.

Until the building of the Market Hall in 1974 all the stalls were in the open air - delightful in good weather and a misery in bad.

At 9.00 am each morning (as had been done since mediaeval times) the Market Bell was rung to signify the opening of trade, and again at 5.00 pm to declare the Market closed. The bell has not been used since about 1970, but it has been

Building the present market in the early 1970s caused great disruption: traders had to move to the shell of what became Littlewoods store on Cheapside, and then to the Court House Station car park until the rebuild was completed.

Today's Market Hall was opened in 1974. By the 21st century however, it was out-of-date and a magnificent design for a new market is envisaged.

Top left, facing page: *A bustling Market Place, May Day Green, circa 1900.* ***Above:*** *An early 20th century stall holder on Market Place.* ***Below:*** *Cheapside showing the covered Market towards the mid-20th century.*

Meanwhile Barnsley retains one of the best markets in England, attracting shoppers from as far afield as Blackpool, Lincoln and Hull.

Many traders of very long standing work in the market, and some have family history of market trading for over 100 years. Edwin Price, greengrocer, is 86 and still assists his son Steve. George 'the Sockman ' Fenton is also in his eighties and now helps his son, Anthony. Michael Hodder similarly assists his son Matthew sell their famous cooked meats.

Another trader of long standing is Peter Kwapisz who deals in curtains and all kinds of fabrics. Peter's father was Polish; he was taken by the Nazis in 1940 and sent to work as a forced labourer in concentration camps. He escaped on three occasions and eventually joined the British Army. After the war he came to England where he was barracked at Smithies, became a miner, and married Jean, a Barnsley girl. Peter Kwapisz

started work in 1966 aged 12, when he had three paper rounds. Being a big lad he found casual work on Barnsley Market the following year: this gave him a good insight as to the pros and cons of market trading. Peter learned his trade in fabrics from an employer, and when he left school to work full time he persuaded his boss to pay him only one day's wage and he would take the rest of his pay in fabric. Being only 16 he could not drive so he persuaded a friend to take him to various markets. He also persuaded his father who was by then suffering from silicosis to open a haberdashery stall. However, Peter's father insisted that he learn 'a good trade' so he joined the Merchant Navy. Less than a year later Peter was back in his beloved market. Over the years he opened shops in various towns, but his heart remained in Barnsley.

Top: Midland Street junction with Queens Road, looking towards Kendray Market and stalls and with the new market and car park under construction. Left: Entrance to Barnsley Market in the 1970s.

largest single project ever to be implemented in the town.

The Council, Yorkshire Forward and the 1249 Regeneration Partnership remain firmly committed to delivering the Barnsley Market Project, despite the difficulties caused by the current financial climate.

The Development Agreement has been extended to allow time to work up revised designs to reflect the changing needs of retailers due to the economic downturn, whilst still retaining a unique and high quality development which will be the iconic jewel in the heart of the town.

Peter Kwapisz was president of the National Federation of Market Traders (Barnsley Branch) for a number of years and always fought hard to support traders when they had had concerns, disputes and grumbles. Along with Geoffrey Blackburn he has been involved in planning the new market for several years, advising 'the powers that be' on market design and logistics to benefit traders and shoppers alike.

The outline planning application for the development is also being extended and has been submitted by 1249.

The cost plan is now being revised and the Compulsory Purchase Order programme is being drafted, however, at this stage there is no firm indication of a date for physical work to begin on site.

The Barnsley Markets project is the centrepiece of 'Remaking Barnsley' which is part of the Yorkshire Forward Renaissance Towns programme, which aims to create urban revitalisation across Yorkshire and the Humber.

Yorkshire Forward combined its assets with those of Barnsley Council to create the opportunity to deliver a world-class shopping and leisure development - the

*Top left: A birds eye view of Barnsley Market in 2010. **Left and above pictures:** Artist impressions of the proposed new-build state-of-the-art Market. Final plans may alter due to the current climate, however, the impressive, world-class shopping and leisure experience Yorkshire Forward and Barnsley Council are planning to bring to the town can be clearly seen in these images.*

Koyo Bearings (Europe) Ltd - New Jobs for Old

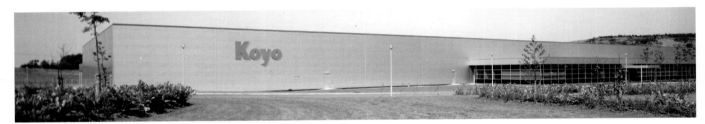

The site on which Koyo Bearings (Europe) Ltd is now situated had, since the mid 19th century, been the site of the Dodworth colliery, a successful coalmine and one of many similar collieries in the South Yorkshire coalfield.

During the long drawn out Miners' Strike of 1984-85 one of the striking miners' biggest worries was that their pits would be closed. And by the late 1980s and early 1990s, this had largely come true. Strange as it now seems, not long before the strike a different future had been proposed, a future that would see the injection of a great deal of money into some Barnsley area pits and an attempt to create the three 'super pits'.

People in Dodworth still speak bitterly about those dashed hopes and about the vast amount of money that was spent on upgrading the three complexes which never came into full use. Instead, the pit shafts were used as dumping sites for the torn down outbuildings, pit heads, and redundant machinery. The shafts were then capped with concrete. Millions of pounds of investment, material, and machinery were literally abandoned, buried into the earth along with the jobs, way of life, and the lost prosperity that they had once represented.

Yet this 'kiss of death' for the coal industry would become the 'kiss of life' for a new enterprise.

In 1986, following the contraction of the coal industry in the region, the Dodworth colliery was closed and the buildings demolished leaving a large area available for new development.

Coincidentally, at the same time Koyo Seiko, of Japan, was looking for a site on which to construct a bearing plant capable of supplying its growing European market.

Established in 1921, with the Head Office in Osaka, Japan, Koyo Seiko had global operations in America, Europe and Asia.

Through maintaining consistently high levels of product quality and performance, Koyo has established itself with automakers

*Top: Koyo Bearings Dodworth. **Above and left:** Two early 20th century views of the Dodworth Colliery, the site now occupied by Koyo Bearings (Europe) Ltd. At the time these photographs were taken it was one of many successful collieries situated in the South Yorkshire coalfield.*

and industrial manufacturers around the world and has attained ISO/TS 16949 certification.

The site of the old colliery at Dodworth proved to be exactly what was required, not least since the site had many attractive attributes: the site was available immediately and had the capacity to be progressively expanded, it had good access to roads, rail and air transport, skilled local people were available with a strong work ethic and who were accustomed to shift working, the land was relatively inexpensive, potential sub-contractors and suppliers were already located in the region, and the new business would be welcomed by the local community which already spoke English the international language of commerce.

Eventually the site was purchased and the official 'Groundbreaking Ceremony' took place on 20 August, 1990.

Council Leader H. Salt gave a heartfelt welcome to the Japanese company "It gives me great pleasure to attend today's historic ceremony with our friends from Koyo Seiko. The symbolic breaking of ground and tree planting have been undertaken with the spirit of mutual co-operation which will ensure that the development here at Dodworth will be a success story for the Council, Company and people of Barnsley."

"At the peak of its working life the colliery at Dodworth employed 1,400 people; sadly employment opportunities in the mining industry have decreased as pits like Dodworth have closed - many of them I have to say unnecessarily. Our task, together with YHDA and Government Agencies, is to ensure that new job opportunities rise from the ashes of the coal industry. We have set ourselves a daunting task over the next 10 years - that is to replace the 20,000 jobs lost from the mining industry. The Koyo development at Dodworth provides a tremendous first step towards achieving

THIS STONE WAS LAID BY MR HIROSHI INOUE PRESIDENT, KOYO SEIKO CO. LTD. ON 8TH OCTOBER 1996

our task. Our friends from Japan bring much needed investment, employment and hope to the area. The Council will continue to provide all assistance at our disposal to help ensure that the Dodworth development is the start of a long, happy and prosperous association with Koyo Seiko Ltd. I am delighted that the Chairman of Koyo Seiko, Mr Uzuhiko Tsuboi, can be with us today. I know that he has travelled a great distance to attend the ceremony."

"This shows how significantly the Company regards its operations in Barnsley. Koyo Seiko is a world famous company which produces high quality products which I know will be competitive in the UK and European Market. I hope that Mr Tsuboi and his colleagues can spend more time with us in the future when we can return their generous hospitality and show them the delights of Barnsley."

Top left: The official Ground Breaking Ceremony on 20 August, 1990. Top right and above: Laying of the foundation stone (pictured above). Below: Construction phases 1, 1991 (top) and 2 in 1996 (bottom) of Koyo Bearings (Europe) Ltd.

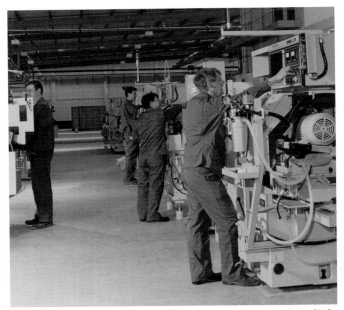

"We have a saying in our country that 'big trees grow from little acorns' - well today we have planted a little tree together which I am sure will flourish in future years as will Koyo Seiko's relationship with Barnsley."

The mention of a 'little tree' was not simply a metaphorical reference to the new factory; after the Mayor, Councillor R Fisher, and Mr Tsuboi had broken the ground a Japanese cherry blossom tree was planted as a symbol of co-operation.

Construction of the factory began immediately, and throughout the following ten months the local population began to see a transformation of the site which had once been occupied by the colliery.

In May, 1991, as the factory neared completion, Mr Tsuboi president of Koyo Seiko paid another short visit during which he was one of the guests presented to Her Majesty the Queen at Barnsley Metrodome.

By the end of July, 1991, the factory was ready to be occupied and on the 5th of August the first group of employees (together with a contingent of Japanese commissioning engineers) moved into the building.

At the same time the first machines began to arrive from Japan and soon all were involved in the installation, commissioning and training process.

By December, 1991, Koyo Bearings (Europe) Ltd (KBE) was ready to despatch the first consignment of bearings to the European Central Office. This coincided with the signing of the 'Enabling Agreement' with the Electrical, Electronic,

Telecommunications and Plumbing Union (EEPTU). This would be one of the final acts which Eric Hammond, General Secretary of the EEPTU, undertook before his retirement.

The official opening took place on 12 June, 1992, and was followed on 22 June by a visit from HRH The Duke of Kent.

Throughout the early part of 1992 more machines lines were added and commissioned until, by late Spring, the factory had six 'TRB' (Taper Roller Bearing) and six 'SBB' (Single Row Ball Bearing) lines.

In July, 1993, the SBB facility was expanded by a further six lines and in July 1995 KBE commissioned its first 'DAC' (Double Angular Contact Bearing) line.

Top left: The first machines arrive at the factory in 1991. *Left:* A staff photo as the first consignment of bearings are dispatched from KBE to the European Central Office. *Above:* In 1991 Mr Tsuboi, president of Koyo Seiko, paid another short visit during which he was presented to Her Majesty the Queen.

made a new start as JTEKT Corporation. As a company centred on the automotive parts business that possesses a firm technological base cultivated through long years of bearing and machine tool manufacturing, JTEKT will aim to win the further trust and high expectations of customers and society.

The JTEKT Corporation owns and operates eighteen bearing plants in seven countries and six R&D Technical Engineering Centres on three continents. Koyo offers innovative solutions to both original equipment manufacturers and aftermarket end users focusing on key markets such as automotive, agriculture and construction, heavy industry, wind power generation, machine tool, electric motor and general machinery.

Left: HRH The Duke of Kent visits KBE on 22 June, 1992. *Below:* A selection of bearings manufactured by Koyo Bearings (Europe) Ltd. *Bottom:* A bird's eye view of the Koyo site in 2010.

Late that same year more SBB and TRB lines were placed in the factory bringing the facility to nine TRB, 16 SBB and one DAC line.

Because of the need to reduce manufacturing costs the decision was made during 1995 to build a small Turning Facility which could produce machined rings from blanks made from steel produced locally. This facility was built during the Autumn of 1995 and commenced production in January, 1996.

Throughout 1995 and the early part of 1996 consideration was given to building a second manufacturing unit to accommodate the diverse requirements of the bearing market. By the middle of 1996 the decision was made to go ahead and the foundation stone was officially laid in October, 1996.

After the foundation stone was laid work began on construction, work which continued throughout the remainder of 1996 and on into the Spring of 1997.

By June, 1997, the building was ready to be occupied and, within the month, the first 'Hub Unit Line' machines arrived from Japan.

The new building was formally handed over to the company on 1 July, 1997.

Koyo Seiko Co. Ltd. and Toyoda Machine Works Ltd. merged on 1 January, 2006, and have

Barnsley College - Education and Inspiration

Barnsley has a proud history in education. That story stretches back to the Victorian era, and to an eagerness for knowledge unparalleled in previous centuries. Today that thirst for knowledge, and the eagerness to provide it, remains undiminished.

The present Barnsley College was formed in 1990, combining the College of Technology, the College of Art, and the Sixth Form College. The setting up of the latter meant the closure, amongst other schools, of Barnsley Girls' High School which had a long history in the town having been established just before the end of the 19th century.

The College of Technology had its origins towards the end of the last century, in classes held under the auspices of the Mechanics' Institute. They were held in the 1880s in what was then known as 'Wright's Warehouses' until, in 1897, the Barnsley and West Riding authorities co-operated in establishing a college with the rather cumbersome title 'Technical School and School of Art'. Its first Principal was appointed in 1906.

In 1912, the year before Barnsley became a county borough, 650 students were in attendance. Throughout the 1920s classes expanded steadily and were taught in scattered premises, taken over to house the various departments, as far apart in distance and suitability as the Harvey Institute and a corrugated iron hut on Queens Road. Since these arrangements were clearly unsuitable, work began on a new College building in 1929. The Mining and Technical College building on Church Street was completed in 1932.

The construction work had cost £80,000, whilst the equipment had cost a further £27,000. The Miners' Welfare Commission contributed £15,000 of this. Shortly after the new College was set up, the School of Art became a separate establishment with its own premises in the Harvey Institute.

Special classes on offer in 1944 were in First Aid, Advanced Gymnastics, Country Dancing, Study of Drama with Practical Work and Psychology. Languages offered included English, German, Spanish, Russian and Latin. In 1946 special classes were extended to include Economics, Speech Training, Musical Appreciation and Gardening Science.

The College of Technology occupied two main sites, the original one on Church Street and the College Extension at the top of Old Mill Lane which was completed

Top: The Belle View site of Barnsley College pictured in 1905. *Left:* A 1964 view inside the Engineering Workshop. **Bottom left and below:** Two of the many college sites in the 1990s, Honeywell (bottom left) and the Huddersfield Road site (below).

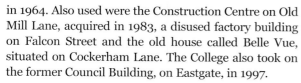

in 1964. Also used were the Construction Centre on Old Mill Lane, acquired in 1983, a disused factory building on Falcon Street and the old house called Belle Vue, situated on Cockerham Lane. The College also took on the former Council Building, on Eastgate, in 1997.

One of the largest employers in the Barnsley area, the College provides almost 700 jobs (full and part time). It was also recognised as an Investor in People in 1995, which was successfully reviewed in 2009.

More recently the College began its property strategy which included building the SciTech Centre, on Falcon Street, which was officially opened in 2004 by Patrick Stewart O.B.E. It also included the selling of the Huddersfield Road site and the Church Street site along with its HE provision, to the University of Huddersfield, which was officially opened as the University Campus Barnsley in May, 2005, by David Blunkett MP.

Since then the College new-build portfolio includes the new motor vehicle workshop on Old Mill Lane and the new Honeywell Sports Centre in 2008.

In 2009 the College started work on the new-build to replace the main campus at Old Mill Lane. Kevin Brennan, Minister for Further Education, Skills, Apprenticeships and Consumer Affairs, visited Barnsley College to celebrate the beginning of the construction work. The 21st century building is designed to be an inspirational learning environment with state-of-the-art facilities, workshops and IT resources. The iconic building is due to be completed in the summer of 2011.

Today the College operates on twelve sites offering a vast choice of courses providing the widest possible range of opportunities for the whole community: sixth-formers, young adults and mature students. Students can learn either full-time, par-time or as part of a work-based learning programme.

From the 19th century to the 21st century tens of thousands of Barnsley people and others from further afield have benefited from not just education but also the inspiration to go on to lead ever more fulfilling lives.

Top left and top right: Two artist impressions of the new-build Barnsley College main campus replacement . Top left is a view from Church Street and top right is a view up Eastgate taken from Falcon Street. **Left:** Honeywell Sports Centre, 2010. **Below:** Barnsley College SciTech Centre pictured in 2010.

Naylor Industries - More Than Just Clay Pipes

In 1890 George Wilfred Naylor started his sanitary pipe business. His salt-glazed pipes for Britain's early sewers still perform well. The business continues today as Naylor Industries Plc.

George Naylor was a railway contractor in his grandfather's firm, Naylor Brothers ,of Scholes. Whilst building the stone railway viaduct at Denby Dale clay deposits were uncovered leading to the foundation of a pipe works. Although the plant has moved down the road to Cawthorne clay pipe manufacture remains an important part of the business.

In 1926, under William Naylor, the company began pre-cast concrete manufacture. Ossett-based subsidiary, Naylor Concrete Products Ltd, now manufactures Britain's most widely specified concrete lintel.

The company's ability to take advantage of the post-war building boom unhappily encountered setbacks as a result of a family tragedy and a disastrous fire. By the 1960s, however, it had re-established itself with the construction of Europe's first tunnel kiln for the volume production of clay drainage - a tradition of investment which the company has been proud to maintain.

Clay's longevity means it remains a popular material, but many other traditional applications for clay pipes have met with competition from plastic.

The company has responded vigorously to such challenges.

Firstly, Naylor has developed new applications for clay pipes.

• Denlok is a high strength pipe for installation by 'trenchless' (No-Dig) methods - a process which minimises surface disruption.

• Hathernware is a range of both pipes and ceramics for the chemical and process industries, with exceptional heat and chemical resistance.

• These developments have been complemented by Band Seal - a universal flexible coupling system.

Secondly, the company has diversified, becoming a major manufacturer of plastic ducting and highway and agricultural drainage-products made not just on the Cawthorne site, but also in factories acquired in Fife and the West Midlands. Closer to its original roots is the development of The Yorkshire Flowerpot Company – Britain's largest manufacturer of clay garden pots.

Finally, the company has developed a strong export market.

George Naylor would have been proud that four generations on, his great-grandson, Edward Naylor, would be heading up a family firm with an annual output of over 20 million metres of pipes.

Top: *George Wilfred Naylor at the turn of the century shunting an engine.* ***Left:*** *Naylor Industries, Clough Green, Cawthorne, Barnsley.* ***Below:*** *Chief Executive, Edward Naylor, receiving an award from the CBI.*

Brian Totty - Signs of Distinction

Brian Totty Signs and Design Ltd, based in Crookes Street, off Summer Lane, was founded in 1978 by local miner's son Brian Totty and his wife Gloria. The firm became a limited company three years later. The company would never have started, however, had it not been for the help of Bill Murphy, an ex-miner disabled through injury, who gave Brian £500 to start on his own.

Brian had learned his trade as a signwriter at the Yorkshire Traction Bus Company. After six years working as company artist for Tesco supermarkets, and then running the sign and poster department at John Green & Son Screenprinters, in Wakefield, Brian decided to step out on his own.

Whilst screen-printing was a large part of the business, sign manufacture was always Brian's main goal.

In the early years Brian worked on his own before moving to a factory unit at Carlton. By then there were eight people employed, not least Brian's wife Gloria. Son Jason and daughter Deborah both joined the family business after leaving school.

Most of the artistic work was done by hand in the early days meaning that Brian was personally behind most of the work in one way or another.

In the late 1980s the company bought its present premises in Crookes Street, Barnsley.

Sadly, Gloria passed away in 2002. Both Jason and Deborah remain very much involved in the business. The company has always kept pace with modern methods of production. That has meant employing young designers with knowledge of digital media and the very latest techniques.

Astonishingly, the firm employs no sales staff. Most clients approach the company themselves, having heard by word of mouth. Staff at Brian Totty are so able and experienced that they often know what the customer wants better than they do themselves!

Meanwhile, with sustained investment and reinvestment over decades, the company continues to grow and aims to move to larger premises in the future.

As for a business philosophy, Brian says that his miner father's words have always stayed with him "Silence is golden; bide thi time, and don't let the buggers get thi dahn".

Top left: Founders, Brian and Gloria Totty in the 1960s. Top right: Early signage. The Webster's sign on the bus was applied by hand by Brian. Bottom left: The company's printing machinery and router. Totty's in-house router bed enables them to cut plastics, foam and aluminium sheets etc. to specific shapes, to create lettering, logos and any other shape customers may need. Above: Brian and Gloria Totty pictured in the 1990s. Below: Totty Signs, Crookes Street, Barnsley.

ACKNOWLEDGMENTS

The publishers would like to sincerely thank a number of individuals and organisations for their help and contribution to this publication.
This book would have been almost impossible without the kind co-operation of the following:

Paul Stebbing, Arhives and Local Studdies Officer, Barnsley Archives and Local Studies for kindly giving his permission to reproduce archive images in this publication.

Chris Sharp, Old Barnsley

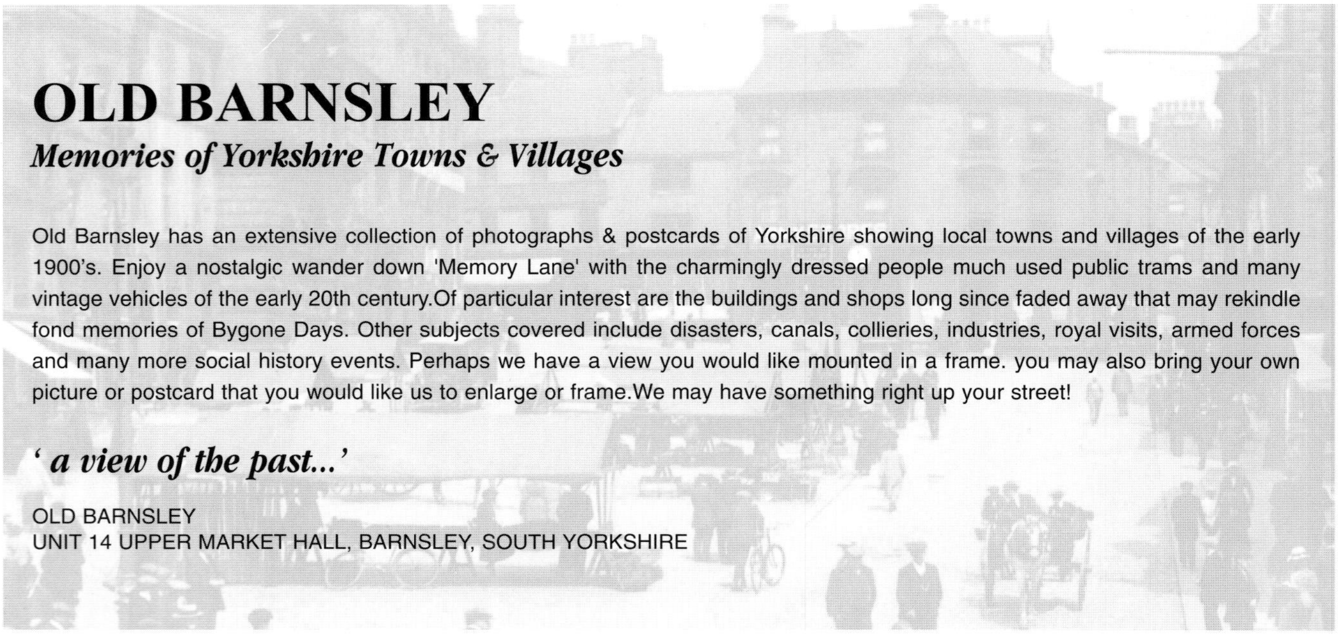

OLD BARNSLEY
Memories of Yorkshire Towns & Villages

Old Barnsley has an extensive collection of photographs & postcards of Yorkshire showing local towns and villages of the early 1900's. Enjoy a nostalgic wander down 'Memory Lane' with the charmingly dressed people much used public trams and many vintage vehicles of the early 20th century.Of particular interest are the buildings and shops long since faded away that may rekindle fond memories of Bygone Days. Other subjects covered include disasters, canals, collieries, industries, royal visits, armed forces and many more social history events. Perhaps we have a view you would like mounted in a frame. you may also bring your own picture or postcard that you would like us to enlarge or frame.We may have something right up your street!

' *a view of the past...*'

OLD BARNSLEY
UNIT 14 UPPER MARKET HALL, BARNSLEY, SOUTH YORKSHIRE